THAT HEAVEN

A Sojourn to Heaven
Living in the Presence of God and Great Ones

Mary Ann Johnston

Tatienne Publishing
Vanderbilt, Michigan

THAT HEAVEN
A Sojourn to Heaven
Living in the Presence of God and Great Ones

All Rights Reserved.
Copyright © 2011 Mary Ann Johnston
v4.0

ORDERS:
http://www.ThatHeaven.com
http://www.OutskirtsPress.com/ThatHeaven

Johnston, Mary Ann, 1940—

THAT HEAVEN
A Sojourn to Heaven
Living in the Presence of God and Great Ones
   1. Religion – Spirituality
   2. Near-Death Experience
   3. Jesus Christ—Apparitions and Miracles
   4. Autobiography

Includes Index.

EDITOR: George O. Johnston

COVER: design & artwork by Robert Bayer & Linda Bayer, RA, of Bayer Essence, Jenison, MI.

CONTACT: Tatienne Publishing, 9543 Rajasi Circle, Vanderbilt, MI 49795-9350. (http://www.ThatHeaven.com)

ISBN: 978-0-9817027-6-6

Library of Congress Control Number: 2011916073

Tatienne Publishing and its logo are trademarks belonging to Tatienne Publishing.

PRINTED IN THE UNITED STATES OF AMERICA

Also by Mary Ann Johnston

SUSTAINED BY FAITH

— ~ —

MESSAGES FROM JESUS

— ~ —

CD ~ HYMNS OF LOVE

DEDICATION

To the One who is many

CONTENTS

POETRY by
MARY ANN JOHNSTON

POETRY by GEORGE JOHNSTON

ACKNOWLEDGEMENTS

There are a few people I'd like to thank: my editor, friend and husband, George, for his dedication, perseverance, and love; Jesus, my dear friend and guide; Yogananda, whom I have come to know; saints and sages who have graced my life; my family and the many dear souls who have given me support and love.

AUTHOR'S NOTE

That Heaven is my third book and brings my life story up to date. When I think back on all I have experienced in this lifetime, I am amazed. It is as if there was an urgency to integrate many experiences in one lifetime, for I have had an abundance of high hills and deep valleys.

Six years ago, in a near-death experience during a heart attack, I visited the heaven I speak of in this book. It was the most profound experience of my life, different from other out-of-body experiences I have had in that my unity with God was complete. I was not an observer separate from God, but was fully united with God. Ego was gone, and my soul had returned to its Source. Upon my return to earth, the longing to go back clung to me like a newborn babe to its mother. I was devastated.

I try to convey my experience of that heaven through poetic imagery. Even so, there are simply no words to describe Oneness in God. Although my mortal mind was not present, through the memory of that experience in my soul I can tell you of it.

As an occupational therapist and healer, I have worked with dying patients and clients and had many opportunities to give words of comfort to those who were at death's door, tell them of a loving, forgiving God, and relate my own experiences in leaving my body to ease their transition. This is one reason I have written this book … I want people to know that there is life after death and there is nothing to fear.

But this book is not only about passing from this world

into another. It is also about realizing God's presence in the here and now. And it is about lifting oneself above the limitations of dogmatic theology. If my beliefs had been constrained by external authority, there would have been little room for spiritual growth.

That Heaven brings to light a fresh, love-filled way of living in God consciousness and communing with God. It is filled with words from Jesus, who wishes to give us teachings that are suited to our understanding in the present age. There are Yogananda's words of encouragement and hope in trying times, Babaji's directives for right living, and experiences I have had that I hope will inspire others to be more open to and accepting of divine awareness, visions, apparitions, miracles, healings, and change. There is so much more in life than meets the eye.

My wish is that what I have written will help you to acknowledge and more fully experience your own spirituality, be more aware of and embrace the presence of God in your life, activate divine energies within yourself, and increase the light in your soul. If you deeply contemplate the truths in this book, they will take on deeper meaning for you and help to relight your memory of Oneness in God.

Chapter One

TRANSCENDING

I gave myself up.
Loosening the bonds of my human form,
I became dancing, multi-hued particles—
a transformation outside myself,
as in a euphoric dream.
Delighting in love,
in that love I was loved.

Spiritual growth is usually unhurried—like a lily quietly unfolding its petals in the light of the sun. At other times, spiritual growth may thunder toward you with a sudden breakthrough into a higher consciousness.

———❀———

S tanding in front of the booth I shared with a daughter at the Body, Mind, Spirit Festival in Warren, Michigan, where I was attempting to sell my first book, *Messages from Jesus*[1], my eyes were drawn to a harnessed, Labrador dog coming down the aisle with his handler. As soon as I saw him from afar, he also saw me, and our eyes met in one of those forever moments. A smile spread throughout my being, like a breeze flowing through, and I knew then that I would be greeting him as though he were a beloved friend. And in this knowing, the spiritual world surpassed the mortal, and time hung in the air as events unfolded in slow motion.

With our eyes locked on one another, fragrant oil suddenly started forming in my hands—real as day—with a fragrance far surpassing that of any flower I have ever known. It was distracting, and I felt as if it were interfering with what was beginning to happen. I struggled with an earth-bound assumption that the strong fragrance might offend the dog in some way. I gave no thought to its significance, its reason for being. Sometimes we struggle when our delusional, earthly ways clash with those of Spirit.

I tried to wipe the fragrant oil on my skirt, only to have it fill my hands, again and again! I kept wiping my hands,

---

1   *Messages from Jesus – A Dialogue of Love,* by Mary Ann Johnston, is primarily a record of conversations that took place during 2002 and 2003 between Jesus and herself. In answering her questions, Jesus helps us to understand profound truths and offers uplifting words of hope and guidance for humanity.
Among the many subjects discussed are: the power of love and forgiveness; how to tell a true master; God as love, light and oneness; communicating with nature; spiritual healing; war and terrorism; how the soul progresses; karma and reincarnation; levels of heaven; final absorption into God.

to no avail. Fragrance filled the air. The dog leaned into his handler and pushed her toward my side of the aisle, dragging her toward me, as if she were nothing. She resisted, and he persisted and won.

As the dog came before me, with his irate handler at his side, my oil-filled hands slowly came out from behind me and went out to him through no effort of my own. He pulled his mistress one last, good pull, so he could reach my hands, sniffed deeply, closed his eyes, backed up on his haunches with his front legs before him, and bowed his head low, between his legs. In soul-orchestration—in time beyond time—I pranamed low before him. . . .

Then out from the depths of a shared eternity, "Bless your heart!" flowed from me in spontaneous verbal blessing, and our joy merged into one love.

And with that, I recognized the spirit of a true friend and teacher from a past life—Sebastian—who, in this life when I was a child, had merged his consciousness with the body of a dog in order to protect me.[2]

The interlude ended in what seemed like an audible snap as his mistress yanked his harness and dragged him off. The moment broken, he went reluctantly.

The oil stopped forming in my hands, its fragrance faded as if it had never been, and my skirt was unstained.

Only then did I look over at my daughter, who was selling essential oils. Caught up with a customer, she had seen the dog and the woman, but was not fully aware of the encounter.

2   Sebastian is mentioned several times in Mary Ann's books *Sustained by Faith* and *Messages from Jesus*.

Soon after, another woman came up to me and said, "I saw that!" She had tuned in to what had taken place.

Thank you, Oh God,
Creator of fragrant oil and
Source of every blessing.
Amen.

Later, I turned and faced the part of the booth where copies of *Messages from Jesus* were on display and contemplated why my huge poster depicting the book cover was not attracting many sales. I suddenly realized that the title, with the word "Jesus" in it, was out of place in this New Age show. There was nothing in the title to convey that my book was a link between Christianity and the New Age. Perhaps those attending the festival associated Jesus with traditional beliefs that no longer, or never, appealed to them, for I saw many of them glance at my poster and rush away, leaving a blur behind them as they distanced themselves from me.

Suddenly, a gentleman stood in front of my booth and started weeping uncontrollably. Tears coursed down his face and his shoulders trembled. He couldn't seem to control his crying. I reached out to comfort him. Then I thought that maybe the huge poster caused his reaction and he wanted a book. I tried to sell him one. Instead he cried out, "No! No! It's not the book, it's you!" Then he faded into the crowd.

I can only surmise that he felt the blissful energy that lingered from the divine encounter with Sebastian.

Chapter Two

TRANSITION

"Before enlightenment he gathered wood
and carried water;
after enlightenment he gathered wood
and carried water."

—Buddhist saying

A h . . . what joys and sorrows we share in the midst of our dream—a dream of our own making. We react to the "slings and arrows of outrageous fortune". We enact a portrayal of who we think others want us to be. We search for God. We search for who we really are. We search for Love.

When souls came into this world to experience it through physical bodies, they were still aware of God. Then, as a result of judgmental and dualistic thinking, they lost this joyful awareness and identified with the body they inhabited and its limitations. For most of them, only a vague memory of God remained. They felt that something was missing and tried to fill the gap with physical pleasures and activities, but of course, nothing else could ever take the place of God. Deep within, many of us long for that Indefinable Source of happiness we once knew.

Most of us do not realize what a great loss this is or even what it is that we long for, but when we experience divine love and bliss, we want more of the same and often begin a conscious search for God.

I believe that every human being is eventually drawn back to God for one or more of the following reasons: curiosity, disillusionment, desperation, a deep longing for God, the gentle promptings of Spirit—the "voice of God" within us.

We have been on a long and winding path for countless lifetimes. In many of them, we only gained a little knowledge of God, or none at all, or we regressed, and in others we were catapulted closer to God. Never were we not on a journey that eventually would bring us home to God.

A spiritual path is a way of life—which often includes spiritual practices—that leads a person toward final liberation in God. In this lifetime, my spiritual path did not begin at Song of the Morning Retreat, where we now live.[3] As a child, I followed in the Christian footsteps of my parents. This Christian upbringing was a good foundation, for Jesus first appeared to me when, at the age of five, I attended my first Sunday school class. From then on, Jesus was my "invisible friend."

Though surrounded by Christian structure, I conversed in heart talk with Jesus, and this became a part of my everyday life with nary a thought to theorize about it. He has been a companion and guide to me all my life.[4]

Heart talk is an aspect of superconscious soul perception, which is the ability to see, hear, and in other ways experience non-physical levels of reality. Communication with Jesus,

3   Song of the Morning Retreat was founded in 1970 by Yogacharya Oliver Black and is based on the work of his guru, Paramahansa Yogananda.
4   In *Sustained by Faith*, Mary Ann tells of her life and experiences with Jesus.

God and nature, for me, feels like a song from my heart flowing through my whole being. Heart talk is an innate ability, awaiting your discovery.

Silently expressing thoughts and feelings from the heart with Jesus was easy for me, and our conversations always concerned only myself, never others. I learned to keep them a secret, because when I spoke of them to others they seemed to shrug it off or turn away in unbelief.

> Joy is there for us
> and we don't laugh.
> Bliss is there for us,
> and we don't feel.
> Spirit speaks to us,
> and we don't hear.
> Miracles happen for us,
> and we don't notice.

Still, I was happy as a child and loved my church family, and my relationship with Jesus sustained me throughout life's challenges.

But after the age of fifty, my life changed dramatically. I was working as a traveling occupational therapist, when suddenly I discovered I had been given the gift of healing others through the power of divine energy and God's grace, and entered a world I was not expecting. It was a calling that filled my life with purpose.

Between traveling assignments, I felt a need to tell my church family about the healings I had witnessed, but many of them did not understand this. They didn't know how to react to me. I felt I didn't belong.

My transformation from non-healer to healer was profound, and I felt restrained by the conservative religious attitudes that surrounded me. I had to make a choice between staying within the confines of the church or accepting whatever God had in store for me. It was difficult to leave it all behind. Many of my friends were church members, and I had been the organist. I gave it all up—every bit of it except the memories—and walked away. In the solace of Jesus' companionship, I simply surrendered to God's will and embraced my new role as a healer.[5]

Since I was recently widowed, my children were grown, and I was traveling as an occupational therapist in three-month settings across the country, I was in an ideal position to utilize the gift of healing and integrate it into my professional work, guided by Spirit. I prayed unceasingly.

> Loving Jesus, hear me. . . .
> Send your healing grace
> into his withered hands.
> Decrease his pain,
> so he may move them
> once again.
>
> ~ ~ ~
>
> Sweet Jesus, hear me. . . .
> Breathe your healing grace through my breath.
> Disperse her agony through my
> breathing out and breathing in.
>
> ~ ~ ~

---

5   More about Mary Ann's healing experiences can be found in *Sustained by Faith* and also in *Messages from Jesus*.

Blessed Jesus, hear me. ...
I see past this ancient man,
this double amputee.
I see a man walking.
You have given me this vision.
Send me all I need to make it so.

~ ~ ~

Gentle Jesus, hear me. . . .
Send your healing grace.
Let me lay my hands, oh so gently,
on this newborn neonate
to give her the will to live,
and stretch, and become uncurled.

~ ~ ~

Compassionate Jesus, hear me. . . .
Send your healing grace thru me,
so I might give comfort
to this broken child.
Fear is written in her body, mind and spirit.
Let my touch be your touch.

~ ~ ~

Gentle Jesus, hear me. . . .
Send your healing love.
Let me hold this beautiful,
Steroid-fed, enlarged babe with your grace.
Nourished by tubes through his heart,
let my embrace heal him through you,
so he may be nourished
with food and love.

~ ~ ~

Comforting Jesus, hear me . . .
Send your healing grace through me
into this dying young mother
so her spirit will be made free.
Help me to comfort her grieving husband
so he may gently let her go
and bravely turn to their sons.

~ ~ ~

Sweet Jesus, hear me, teach me, move me,
to touch a stranger's pained knee,
or a friend's headache,
or a grandson's tear,
or a puppy's cry,
or a flower's wilting.

Thank you, Sweet Jesus,
for your comforting presence
and answering my prayers.

———————

In 1996, while I was on a three-month assignment in Albuquerque, New Mexico, I took a trip to see what was on the other side of the Sandia and Manzano mountains. I rose early and packed an overnight bag and some water and headed for the mountains. It was Thanksgiving Day.

I couldn't help but think about the nursery rhyme that I sang as a child.

The bear went over the mountain,
The bear went over the mountain,
The bear went over the mountain,
To see what he could see.
And all that he could see,
And all that he could see,
Was . . . the other side of the mountain,
The other side of the mountain.
The other side of the mountain
Was all that he could see.

I had planned to do some exploring. The map showed a few ruins on highway 14, which would eventually take me into the beautiful, mountain-resort village of Ruidoso, and then to the Mescalero gambling resort, "Inn of the Mountain Gods", where I was to meet with some healer friends for a Thanksgiving dinner.

I started out on I-40, the expressway through the pass between the mountains. It was nearly deserted. I left I-40 and started south on highway 14. The road wound through villages with opulent and crude homes nestled within the mountains, under the bright New Mexico blue sky. The wind was cold as I made my way slowly, savoring the views. Nothing was going to rush me that day.

I arrived at the Salinas Pueblo Mission, which is a National Monument, named for the salt lakes at the base of the mountains. The Spaniards used Indian labor to bring the salt down the Rio Grande River to where it was hauled in carts to silver mines in Chihuahua, Mexico. Salt was crucial to the process of silver smelting.

What remained to be seen and was not buried by centuries of wind-blown sand was the skeleton of the Spanish church. I explored the area and the church. Since it was Thanksgiving, I was the only visitor at these National Park sites.

Then I drove to the Gran Quivera Ruins and visited a ruin that had been inhabited by the Tompiro Indians for nine centuries. I was alone to explore—accompanied by a howling wind and helped by a blue-colored bird, which guided me here and there. I could feel the Spanish influence/interference. Little is known of the history of the people as the ruins are still mostly buried. Many mounds of maze-type pueblos were protruding partially into the air.

How could these ancient people survive drought and famine in the distant past, yet could not survive in the end? What survival techniques and customs were lost or not allowed by the Spanish Church?

I felt as though I was an intruder. I was almost finished with my walkabout when strong feelings of sorrow hit me. I sat down on a low adobe wall, which would have been the last wall built, wall upon wall, upon wall. The blue bird settled on a tree branch.

The earliest pueblos supposedly were built in five or six concentric circles and contained up to 200 rooms. In that early phase, the masonry work was very durable since a source of yellow clay was nearby. When they were excavated, these pueblos were found to be intact. After they had been filled in from years of blowing sand, they were topped with round to rectangular pueblos. But the new rockwork was of poorer quality, because the source of yellow clay had become hidden by the sand.

I began to mourn the fact that once the Spaniards occupied the area, the decline of the Indians began. It seemed as though this happened either because of greed or sickness brought by the intruders, drought, or religion replacing native customs. I could see them trying to resist and then giving in.

I was about to say a prayer, when the New Mexico wind became still. The blue bird stopped its song. The silence fed my prayer for the lost peoples of these pueblos, and I thanked them for allowing me the honor of visiting with them in their ancient home. I could sense them as if they were there as they were in the far past. I communicated with them through heart talk, apologizing for the changes brought to the natural order of their culture. I apologized for any damage my intrusion might have caused and prayed for them to be at peace within their sky-heaven.

I felt like I was in a hushed vacuum, in tune with the past, one with the Indians in spirit, not of this time. In a spiritual trance and far removed from duality, their energy penetrated my heart and depressed my spirit at the same time. Dark nights' secrets and sadness lingered within. My eyes filled with tears while visions passed before me, one after the other, of what swept their heritage away—exploitation, disease, hunger, defeat. I apologized for it all and cried aloud, as a mother would for a lost child.

I drew in my breath and the vision stopped, time stopped. A whisper of wind entered my right ear, and with no room for misinterpretation, I felt a "Thank you!" Then, another whirlwind at the top of my head caused me to stand and lift my arms to dance in communion with the spirits, in cadence with my slowed, drumming pulse.

A welcoming, peaceful feeling came over me. Then the wind picked up its mighty force as if it were more than wind. The blue bird sang. I meditated for a while, then went on my way.

From there I drove up into Alto, New Mexico, a 7,300-foot elevation, and then a short drive to Ruidoso. In the clear blue sky, I could see Sierra Blanc at 12,000 feet—old granite baldy—sitting spectacularly at the head of the White Mountains, an awesome sight.

I met my friends for dinner at the Inn of the Mountain Gods on the Mescalero Reservation. We feasted for two hours. What fun and joy filled our hearts and good food our bellies.

During dinner, snow began to move in and, by the time we were finished, it was floating downward through the troposphere in a haze of microscopic stars that touched everything with glittering diamonds.

I left to go down the mountain while the going was good. By the time I reached a mesa, at 6,500 feet, the flakes were silver dollar-sized lace. They were so beautiful that I didn't think about what might happen going across a nearly isolated mesa in a snowstorm. I followed a car ahead of me or I might not have been able to see the road.

After a while, I realized I had better look at the map for shelter. I saw that there was a small village up ahead, Mountainaire, and I hoped there would be a room for me for the night. Luckily, I made it to the village, plowing through snow, and found a poorly heated motel room, but was provided with plenty of blankets to wrap up in.

The next morning, the sky was clear blue, as if nothing had happened, but the ground was covered with very deep, brilliant, diamond-laden snow, lying quietly, awaiting my next adventure.

Still up in the mountains on the mesa, I started out slowly, taking in the beauty of it all. My Buick Roadmaster plowed through snow all the way down the mountain to the freeway, only to find out that the freeway was closed. Once again, I was stranded, but there just happened to be a motel at the intersection. Finally, the next day, I was able to make my way back to Albuquerque for work.

After three years of travel, working as an occupational therapist/healer in medical facilities and nursing homes, mainly in the Southwest, Jesus urged me to return to my hometown in Michigan, and within a short time, I had a profound experience that changed me and altered my life, just as becoming a healer had done three years previously.

———— ⊗⊗⊗ ————

On New Year's morning, 1998, I had a powerful awakening, brought on by a kundalini energy flow, so fierce that I was hospitalized and then in therapy for months. Normally, a spiritual awakening does not have harmful effects, and in the past, I often had experienced bliss when my pelvic floor would clamp shut and energy would shoot up my spine. But when it happened this time, the energy that flowed through my spine, brain, and entire body was so intense it opened me to deeper levels of spiritual awareness. It was as if layers of veil between the world of ordinary human perception and the spirit world had been lifted.

My physical body and cognition were affected as though I had suffered a stroke. But all that the medical tests indicated was an increase in brain activity.

I wrote poetry to describe and express what I saw, felt and heard as I began to experience, ever more deeply, the divinity in nature and an expanding awareness of oneness in God. As a result of this awakening, I am less affected now by the delusive thought that where I end the rest begins. It's all one!

At some point, while yet in rehabilitation, I was told of Song of the Morning Retreat. And, through inner prompting from Jesus, I felt an urgency to go there that I could not deny. Without consent from my caregivers, I drove the long distance anyway, and because of my decreased strength, it was not easy for me to walk through the snow from building to building. I often had to lie upon the snow to rest.

Following my initial visit, I was moved to go for another and another . . . and eventually doors opened up for me for a job in the area and a place to stay. Jesus and all my spirit friends were a big part of my life, and I was filled with gratitude for all the lessons and blessings I was receiving.

After some time, I met George at the Retreat, and we married in the year 2000. A year later, we were the first to build a home in the new Clear Light Community within the eight-hundred-acre, forested Retreat.

Here, I am free to worship at home or with others, as I wish, and meditate in my own way. I love the acceptance that abounds here at the Retreat; individual differences are respected and there is a spiritual energy that sustains me.

Just as birds of a feather flock together, people with similar soul traits are drawn to certain teachings and teachers, and like to pray, sing and worship together. Yet, each follower of a spiritual path or religion will, to some degree, implement its teachings in their own unique way, because each of us is an individual soul and has a unique personal relationship with God, as well as different strengths and weaknesses.

Nevertheless, all spiritual paths have the same purpose: to help us grow spiritually and realize God. We call God by different names and say different prayers, but God is love. Connecting with God is the common constant uniting all true spiritual paths and religions.

Although I became disenchanted with the rigidly held dogma and conservatism of organized religion, I am not down on religions that teach love, for they help people in many ways. Christianity was a good foundation for me and provided me with a way of worshipping God.

If you feel a need for religious structure, it can be of help, as long as it does not keep you from expanding your horizons and moving on if you ever wish to do so.

A religion should not block your way if more is opened up for you, but should honor whatever path you choose to take.

Some see our holy books –
Our covenants, both old and new –
As perfect, free from
Human limitation.

But scholars know these books to be
Both human and divine
And that translations of key words
Are sometimes far from certain.

Moreover, some religious teachings are
Approximations of the truth.
As mankind grows in wisdom
These teaching often change.

Old-time religion saw a wrathful God
And evil, guilt and sin.
It dwelt on retribution
And what a fix we're in.

Now, many see with eyes of soul
And know a loving God.
They emulate the lives of saints
And tread the paths they trod.

And through deep meditation,
Self-discipline and love,
They open inner portals
That lead to heaven above.

For God is known by higher consciousness alone,
And heard and felt and seen
In the beauty of Creation
And in stillness deep within.

And just behind this world exist
God's holy light and sound,
And hidden truth in timeless realms
Where love and bliss abound.

—George Johnston

Chapter Three

SONG OF THE MORNING

Prayer should take into consideration the past also.
Pray for the past that it not affect today disharmoniously.
Praying for the conceived past is as important
as praying for the probable future.

Years ago when I was a small child, I went to a day camp
for Girl Scout Brownies. It was held in a forested area.
I had always lived in a town and not had the opportunity
to experience a forest, although I had seen wooded areas in
books and while riding in a car. Even on my grandparents'
farm there were few trees, as it was mostly planted fields.

Upon arrival at the camp, it was the smell of the forest
that hit me first— the all-inclusive, aromatic blend of all that
dwelled within the forest. Much to my delight, I was able to
sort out and enjoy the unique smell of the trees, pine needles,
soil, and wild flowers . . . the feel of bark and moss . . . sounds
of birds and wind in the trees . . . and the sun peeking through
and lighting up this and that and causing dancing shadows.
It was as if they had never existed before for me, and now I
was a part of it all. I had to touch and smell everything.

Then there were the colors, from the ground to the canopy of the trees, where the bright, blue sky filled in the empty
spaces.

There were squirrels, and a myriad of bugs to study here

and there. It was like an awakening, realizing how alive that forest was—but I didn't think about this at the time, it just was—and I ran from one thing to another, playing in the moment, as if I had found long-lost friends.

I never had to be told what to do when I went outdoors as a child. There was so much to do. My job was to wash dishes, and I couldn't wait for my parents and brother to eat the last of their food so I could whisk the dishes out from under their noses, often with a reprimand, to get them done. Then I could go out to play.

Today when you tell children to go outside and play, they often say, "What can we do outdoors?" There are vital energies in nature—in fresh air, sunlight, plants and trees. Television and electronic games and entertainment often keep them indoors, away from the healing power in outdoor exercise and play.

My husband, George, and I live in a community in a forest, across the river from the Song of the Morning Retreat. Every time I walk out our sliding glass doors into our garden in the woods, I still feel that same, wonderful, fresh delight that I felt back then—at one with nature and the animals in its keep.

The Retreat is in the upper part of lower Michigan. It has a vortex of welcoming energy emanating from its very heart and is ruffled only by human frailties, which sometimes rock the Retreat's foundation.

Song of the Morning Retreat was founded in 1970 by Yogacharya Oliver Black[6] and was based on the work of

6   Yogacharya Black was a direct disciple of Yogananda. In other words, he

his guru, Paramahansa Yogananda.[7] Yogacharya had established the Retreat in order to further the Self-Realization Fellowship (SRF) teachings of Yogananda.

Yogananda's and Yogacharya's presence in Spirit is evident to me at the Retreat, as if . . . as if they are alive and watchful.

Several years after Yogacharya's death in 1989, the board of directors governing the Retreat appointed another direct disciple of Yogananda, who had been a friend of Yogacharya, as spiritual director. For almost ten years, he introduced various spiritual paths at Song of the Morning, which had the effect of weakening the Retreat's focus on the SRF teachings and gurus.

The various teachings that were presented diluted those of Yogananda and produced a chaotic energy at the Retreat, for many members considered themselves disciples of Yogananda and didn't want to pursue other spiritual philosophies, practices, and gurus.

Yogacharya used to joke about the dog with a bone in its mouth, who saw another bone and went after it. In so doing, the dog dropped the bone from its mouth and didn't get the other bone either.

The point he was making is that, once someone formally

---

became a disciple while the master was still in a physical body.

7   Paramahansa Yogananda, a Self-realized master from India, lived in the United States from 1920 until his passing in 1952. He taught yoga meditation, for stilling the mind and communing with God, to many thousands of disciples and students. He lectured, wrote extensively, and established in Los Angeles the headquarters of his international society, Self-Realization Fellowship (SRF), whose monastic disciples publish his writings, guide members in their practice of his teachings, and oversee temples and meditation centers around the world.

enters into a sacred relationship with an enlightened being, accepting him or her as their guru, they should practice that guru's teachings wholeheartedly to the best of their ability and not dilute their efforts by pursuing other spiritual teachings. It may take years of concentrated effort to understand the teachings of a spiritual path like Yogananda's, to become proficient in its disciplines, and to attune one's heart and mind to the thoughts and wishes of one's guru.

Since they were not interested in other teachings and teachers, many who had been introduced to Yogananda's SRF path by Yogacharya stopped coming to Song of the Morning. Constant vigilance was required of those who continued to come, to be able to keep Yogananda in their hearts and minds and practice his teachings.

Then, about a year or two before the spiritual director retired, he changed course, and in January, 2003, he wrote to the board of directors:

> *"I feel that the time has come to eliminate the multiple teachings that have been promulgated here and to have a one-pointed focus on Master Yogananda's teachings and his philosophy of life."*

What is different now (at the time of this writing) from when I first came to Song of the Morning is that the Sunday services are Yogananda's teachings with nothing added, and although people from other traditions come here to teach different holistic and spiritual methods of healing and self-help (mainly to their own groups and the public), only the SRF path is presented at our services and meditations.

This has helped to fulfill the director's parting wishes and also those of the Retreat's founder, Yogacharya Oliver Black, who stated in his will that Song of the Morning existed for the purpose of furthering the teachings of Paramahansa Yogananda and Self-Realization Fellowship, together with the establishment of a World Brotherhood Colony (a term coined by Yogananda for the self-sustaining, spiritual communities that he envisioned would spring up around the world).

My husband, George, tells me that Yogacharya Oliver Black often quoted Jesus' admonition that the branch must be connected to the vine, the vine being the devotee's divinely ordained source of guidance and truth.

As the branch
cannot bear fruit by itself,
unless it abides in the vine,
neither can you, unless you abide in me.[8]

While writing *Sustained by Faith* from our home in the Clear Light Community, commenting on my first visits to Song of the Morning—when some teachings that were being presented were obscuring those of Yogananda and making me uneasy—Jesus instilled in my heart:

"Patience, Dear One. The structure at Song of the Morning is hidden for now and, when it is found, it will be like welcoming home a lost child."[9]

8   John 15:4
9   *Sustained by Faith*, p. 153.

Chapter Four

COMPASSION

I dance as if I were of the
northern lights, not mortal;
colorful, alive, flowing
in syncopation with
Mother Earth and Father Sky.

I often stood in the back entryway of my childhood home, in the wintry cold, bundled up in winter garb, gazing at Jack Frost's art work on the frosted window-pane of the door. It was as if nature was thinking spring, for the art work mimicked leaves and ferns in lovely crystal patterns. Each new, frosty day, a different nature pattern appeared, never the same, sometimes one on top of another. It was, for me, a simple miracle, mingled with mystery in my young mind, for I could never catch Jack Frost at work.

Several winters ago, George and I looked out the sliding glass doors in our living room upon an idyllic, wintry landscape. You know, the kind where the sun is shining on snow and ice-covered branches, and everything glistens and sparkles like diamonds. It took our breath away.

George was about to exclaim some wonderful words about the scene, when I was moved to remind him, "Don't think, just look," just as we both normally do when meditating on the beauty in nature. Wiping all thoughts away as they came up, there was a period of deep silence in the looking.

The mind's ever-flowing thoughts interfere with con-
templation of nature. Thus, I have to remind myself, "Don't
think, just look", as I look deep into the woods or up into the
sky, or at sunlight peeking through the leaves, or moonlight
dancing on water, or at any of the wonders of God's creation.
Very soon I feel myself sinking into deep peace. Even then,
I don't think about the peace, and the beauty and bliss take
over. It may last for some time or it may be just a passing
moment. Such peaceful interludes make it easier to handle
whatever difficulties come one's way.

Early in 2005, George and I left the Michigan winter behind and drove to Tucson, Arizona, where I took a
three-month job in a large hospital as a traveling occupational therapist.[10] Our apartment was east of the city, near
the Saguaro National Park. We spent a considerable amount
of time picnicking in the park and enjoying the large saguaro
cacti and other desert plants and animals—so different from
those in Michigan.

Spring is a wonderful time to be in the desert. One week-
end, as we traveled to the Grand Canyon, the desert floor
and the highway meridian were blanketed with royal-blue
lupine, desert marigolds, and flowering cacti, as far as you
could see. It was a lovely prelude to the vast expanses and
grandeur of the Grand Canyon.

---

10   A traveling therapist holds a temporary position, often lasting only three
      months. They are needed when a facility has to replace someone on mater-
      nity or medical leave, or during a seasonal increase in population.

I love to sit close to the canyon's edge and watch the changing cloud-shadows creep over the canyon walls, and the sun, slowly moving across the sky, shine into the depths of the canyon. The sun lights up the colorful rock layers, in a myriad of shades of orange, tan, red, cream, green, gray and purple. Each layer, sculpted by natural forces, is made up of a different kind of mineral deposited over eons of time.

Where sound and silence are united,
in soundless song I sing God's name
in concert with all nature's glory.
One in all, it is the same.

And after a day thus spent, when evening shadows quietly fall, the sun sets over the canyon, giving solemn rise to red, purple, orange and golden colors in the clouds and sky. People rush to find the best location to catch the last vestige of the sun as it hesitates on the brink of the earth before disappearing over the horizon.

During my hospital assignment, I had the same dream three nights in a row—that I would be running someone over with my car. The following week, I wanted to go into a little strip mall, but all the parking was taken. I remembered that there was parking in the back, so I went around the buildings. I came to a pile of trash spilled over from a dumpster, blocking entry to the parking. I could have gone through it but, intuitively, I thought I should check it out; besides, I didn't want a flat tire. What I found under the newspapers was a sleeping, homeless person. I might have run him over!

Carondelet Health Network is Southern Arizona's oldest and largest non-profit healthcare provider. It is the mission of Carondelet Health Network to provide for the health care needs of the community, to embrace the whole person in mind, body and spirit, and to serve all people with dignity. Founded by the Sisters of St. Joseph of Carondelet, its health facilities were originally established in France.

I worked in St. Joseph Hospital, a part of this network, and was soon set in my place. As a traveler, I was expected to make it worth their while to have me there. They pay a lot of money for traveling therapists, and a big percentage of time on the job has to be for billable services. I was not allowed to go to meetings, except during a lunch break or off hours. I can understand that; money is important in a charitable hospital, and there were many patients who could not pay for care. Some were street people and some were illegal immigrants who had medical difficulties while crossing the desert attempting to come to the States to work.

One sweet soul, who had made this trip from Mexico, illegally, for several years with other family members to work our fields, suffered a stroke in the desert. Fear of deportation drove his family on, and he was left behind. Border patrols were alerted and he was brought to the hospital. He could not speak English. Upon eventual discharge from the hospital, they took him back to the Mexican border. His home was in southern Mexico, and he had no means to get himself from the border to his home. His family was poor. Staff and others did what they could to make his trip possible.

I remember patients from off the streets of Tucson and how they would be worried about their stash that they had hidden in the city, hoping no one would steal it while they were laid up in the hospital. Some liked living on the street; they had their friends and knew where to go for a handout and shelter. For some, and they were of all ages, there prevailed an aura of hopelessness. Others were clearly mentally ill and found comfort or conflict in each other. In days past, society would have cared for these people in live-in facilities.

Now there are more and more desperate people from all walks of life—adults and children—living in cars, on the streets, under the streets in tunnels, with relatives, or in tent cities, because of inability to cope in the world, lost jobs, or lost families and homes.

I once worked with a physical therapist from Calcutta, India. He told me some horrible things about life there, and what people suffer through. I said in concern, "I can just imagine how bad it must be." Near shouting, he immediately, with intense feeling said, "No you cannot! You cannot imagine how bad it is there!" He is right. I never say, "I can just imagine" anymore, because I am not in another person's shoes. I cannot truly know or even imagine their pain, their sorrow, or their despair.

One of my street patients had been left with both receptive and expressive aphasia, after a stroke. He could not understand what he was hearing and could not express himself so people could understand him. He must have felt as if cast amidst strangers in a foreign land, with a foreign language and no way to get one's needs expressed—even gestures were not understood by either party.

He had no identification and had been picked up on the street. Eventually a friend came looking for him, having missed him. Through his friend, we found out our patient had been an avid guitar player. He had been trying to get across to us that he had lost his guitar and didn't know where to find it. A search began by street people, for they loved him and missed his music. I never heard if they found the guitar or, if they did, whether he was able to pick up where he left off, to play it.

It takes resilience for those blessed with visions of the world as it could be—healed and whole, with love as the governing principle in every person and institution—to remain cheerful, hopeful, and grounded in the present, while doing their best, calmly and compassionately, to help others less fortunate.

Compassion is not wholly contained in just inactive empathy. Compassion can come to the aid of a motorist in trouble or pick up a lost animal and care for it. Compassion can serve food to the hungry. Compassion can provide a bed and blanket. Compassion can soothe the sorrowful with music or kind words and warm their hearts with a smile. Compassion can pray for the highest good of one or many. Compassion gives lovingly, creatively, generously, and without expectation.

In contrast, there is the indifference that arises when the natural, loving impulses of the heart are blocked. Those who are indifferent to the needs of others think only of their own comfort, while sitting in a warm home, with food in the refrigerator, hot water when needed, and income to provide for more than basic needs.

I enjoyed the people who worked in the hospital. Spanish-speaking nurse aides were constantly drilling me, trying to teach me Spanish. Coming around a corner or out from a room, they would surprise me with a Spanish greeting and expected an instant Spanish response. I was terrible at it. Most often we ended up laughing.

Initially, casually speaking of myself as a healer with my supervisor and staff, I met with opposition. Talk of healing was frowned upon by my supervisor and some fellow therapists. So, after my initial disclosure, I did not mention healing to them again. However, I am never intrusive, and most healing is done as I separate myself into two entities; one, the therapist going about my duties, the other, the mind of my soul, in healing conversation with God for others. They would never have understood that.

I am not guided to everyone for healing. However, when God directs me to do so, I do everything in my power to follow through. I have learned that if I don't follow through, I am distressed for quite some time.

One day I did an evaluation of an elderly woman. I felt a strong inclination to do more . . . to heal, to comfort, to give her more time. Restricted as I was, I could only inwardly pray for her to be healed if it were for her highest good. Healing is often instantaneous, but I felt she required more, and I left feeling very unsettled.

I took her chart from the nurse's station and went to a little room to study it, to continue in my evaluation of her. A priest walked in and sat across from me at the table. He wanted the chart I was studying when I was through.

When I was finished, I closed the chart, rested my arms on it, looked into his eyes, and with deep feeling, said, "I am a healer, and I felt a strong intuition to use laying on of hands for this woman, but I don't feel staff would understand what I am doing and I am afraid that I would lose my job if I did so. It's tearing me apart."

After talking to him further, the priest emphatically said, "You do what you are moved to do anytime you want. If anyone confronts you, tell them Father ___ said you could do this!"

I was speechless! I could not do what was in my heart, so Spirit set this meeting up. What else could it be? Bless Father ___! He stood for what the hospital proclaimed as its mission—to embrace the whole person in mind, body and spirit.

I revisited this woman in her room. I took her hand and held it so that she could not only hear me, but could feel my words and prayers for her through her hands and heart, simple as that. Healing not only embraces the physical, but the mind and soul as well.

From then on, I felt an inner freedom to address callings from Spirit to help people on their road to healing, and many private moments opened up with patients for healing thoughts, comfort, prayer, and laying on of hands, none of which interfered with my regular duties.

The hospital offered a class: "Introduction to Spirituality", and the first session fit my lunch schedule. While attending it, I had an opportunity to tell everyone that I thought all the wonderful sunshine surely had a positive effect on people in Tucson. I was finding sweet people everywhere—children were well mannered, everyone was friendly, and I didn't see any road rage. As soon as I said this, other participants jumped in with many contrary statements. It felt like an encroaching darkness attempting to come over me, but I wouldn't let it.

We create our world through the lens of our thoughts and feelings. I realized more fully from the ensuing conversation, that negative thinking and judgment keep us from seeing the good in ourselves and the world. They also make it difficult for us to experience oneness because they perpetuate the illusion of separation.

If you criticize or judge something, in your mind you have separated yourself from it. If you do this toward others, you shut your heart down and create disharmony, limiting your ability to empathize with and understand them. The idea of separation keeps us from seeing the oneness behind the relativities and contrasts of the world, adding darkness into the world and layer upon layer of veil to the almost-universal delusion that we are separate from God.

Appreciation and love open the heart and reveal our divinity and oneness with each other and God, while criticism and condemnation make it difficult for us to realize that we are all connected and that every person, in essence, is divine. For all of us, regardless of what we have done, are immortal souls, created by God from out of God's own spiritual substance. As the Bible states and great masters like Jesus have confirmed, we are made in the image and likeness of God.

If you would forget everything you know about a person's past and just stay in the present moment as you look at or talk with them, you wouldn't judge them. By focusing on the good you see in them, in the present moment—the now—and forgetting all else, not only are you able to empathize with them, but your positive thoughts help to lift them up. Moreover, through wisdom and love, you are able to look beyond the evil in your own or someone else's past and accept the fact that behind one's mortal mind, deluded by false concepts and influenced by selfish motives, lies their perfect, divine essence—the eternal Self.

In knowing this, it is easier to love and forgive, rise above guilt, condemnation and hate, and become more compassionate.

The concepts of sin—guilt, condemnation, retribution, vengeance, damnation—blind many of us to the truth of our inherent divinity. These concepts were established in the distant past to enforce moral behavior, but they obscure the innocence of the immortal, everlasting Self—beyond the stain of sin or guilt—which dwells with us as the essence of our soul. The Self is one's true identity; not the outer personality, which changes and does not last forever.

Often people are excessively hard on themselves, constantly judging themselves and others. In *Messages from Jesus*, Jesus tells us: *"God is a loving God. God does not judge. God may intervene to make change in your life and others', but God does not judge. Mankind must be forgiving, so no karmic debt is created. If people truly forgave their selves and others, they would be so full of light it would feel as if the weight of the world was lifted from them. They would simply sin no more."[11]*

Both Jesus and Yogananda tell us that sins are spiritual mistakes, nothing more and nothing less. Instead of constantly judging ourselves and others, we should resolve to do better in the future, try to repair any damage that may have been done, forgive, and move on. For, as God loves us and sees the perfection in everyone, so should we.

In time, each of us will experience our perfection and immortality. We will realize the Self. In that blissful epiphany, we will discover that we are, and always have been, united with each other in the oneness of Spirit, the oneness of God.

---

11 *Messages from Jesus,* Third edition, p. 39.

GUILT

Some say . . .
there is no guilt . . .
there never was.

There is only innocence,
interwoven in our own, perceived,
personal realities.

To change the wrong,
the concepts of sin,
is to grow in the light
of The One.

To understand The One
is to let go of the ego and to meld
with all the universes
and into each other.

I say, "Welcome. . . ."
This freedom
to do no wrong
frees my soul to be in the world
above no one and below no one.

It urges me to do only good.
It creates in me a resurrection
to the surface,
whereupon I can blossom
like the lotus into my truth.

Chapter Five

INCREASE THE LIGHT

This little light of mine, I'm gonna let it shine.
This little light of mine, I'm gonna let it shine,
let it shine,
let it shine,
let it shine![12]

One very lovely, clear, blue-sky morning, brilliant light, more than sunlight, seemed to be chasing the shadows as it slowly appeared in our garden. I stood to greet it, and the weeds I had been pulling gave off a sweet fragrance as they dropped at my feet.

Pulsating rays of light spread outward further and further, encompassing me and the whole of the garden, taking up the forest, the air, the shadows. My breath was on hold as I became one with the patterns of light, shimmering, descending, and entering the garden. In slow motion—in divine expression—the brilliant light spread outward, like particles of praise, into the forest and sky.

I was simply an observer of life, watchful.

Slowly, breath came back to me, duality revisited me, and I returned to body consciousness. Everything was still lit up, outlined in brilliance, and remained so for some time.

---

12   "*This Little Light of Mine*", a gospel children's song, Harry Dixon Loes (1895-1965) c.1920.

I was left with an all-encompassing feeling of having had the Holy Spirit, once again, lay claim on me, engulfing and assimilating me in brilliant, divine love. I felt it was a sign to start singing, and I began to sing the sacred Gayatri mantra.

We all dwell in the Holy Spirit, unaware, yet at times It makes Itself known without beckoning and surprises us when we least expect it.

This phenomenon of brilliance seeing has occurred in many instances throughout my life. It comes at unexpected times, in unexpected places, in everyday life.

If you have never seen divine light, you may have wondered, "What is this light? Why can't I see it?" Some people see white light, and some see colors or golden light. Some see nothing but can sense or feel the light. Some see auras and some don't. Some feel auras and some don't. Some see, feel or sense nothing. Whether you experience God's light or not, it is there . . .

> Close your eyes. . . .
> Settle yourself. . . .
> Take a deep breath. . . .
> Sigh it out. . . .Relax. . . .
> Drop your shoulders. . . .

> With every breath imagine
> within your heart—Love . . .
> as a spark of light expanding within.
> Surrender yourself to the power of love.

Feel the light brighten and grow . . .
growing, growing, ever brighter . . .
filling you with warmth. . . .
With every breath, hold the light.

Do this until,
in the hush of an abiding moment,
you feel a glowing smile within,
expanding with every breath you take,
cleansing all there is of you
in a bliss bath
of love-filled light.

In the Beatitudes, Jesus spoke to a multitude. . . . He was not speaking only to His disciples. He said: "*You are the light of the world.*"[13] He was urging them to shine the light of their souls before others—to make manifest to others the divinity within themselves through the example of their good actions—and thus glorify God.

Just think of the moral responsibility that comes from this. The world is dependent upon us to shine our light with goodness and love.

———✤———

We have all seen people full of love and compassion. They radiate a powerful energy of love and joy. This energy is the light of God within them. The more forgiving and loving you are, the more you shine; and the more love,

---

13   Matthew 5:14.

light, and joy you have in your life, the more you touch others.

I was walking through a huge mall one fine spring day with my daughter. Within the oncoming crowd I saw one such person. She did not stand out because of her hair or clothing. She was simply one of many. I could feel her energy 100 feet away. Her eyes met mine, and the closer we came toward one another, the stronger the energy was. We were both smiling, full of joy, as we passed each other and went our way—no words were spoken, no words were needed.

My daughter, walking next to me, said, "Mom, I saw that."

Recently George and I went out for breakfast. In the restaurant a television program was showing, but was muted while a radio was blasting. The program was of a minister preaching to his congregation. Neither George nor I are drawn to television ministries, but as I watched, I said to him, "Look at that minister; he shines. He doesn't put on any airs." We both watched for a while, giving the blasting radio a back seat. Later I said, "He doesn't have much ego about him at all. He looks sincere in his message," all while not hearing a sound. It was very moving. His very essence carried the message he gave.

This energy is of love and light, and the more non-judgmental and loving we are, the more we are aware of God as love and light within us. Those who bring sunshine into the lives of others cannot keep it from themselves, for giving and receiving are reciprocal. And each person's happiness is important to everyone else, for we are all one in Spirit and share the same collective experience.

In *Messages from Jesus,* Jesus said,

"Everyone shines their light, some brighter than others. How do you think it is that you can send others light if you didn't have it inside of yourself?"

Then I said to Him, "I never thought of that. People often ask me how to shine light on others. It is difficult to explain."

And Jesus replied, *"One simple way to explain it would be to tell people to smile on self and others."*[14]

I love this; a simple smile can be like a light switch. When you smile at someone, they light up. And when others smile on you, you feel lighter. That is the light, and it rids you and others of darkness. In *Messages* I wrote:

"When His Holiness Cealo, a Buddhist monk, came to visit, he told me to simply heal souls. He did not give me directions nor did I ask for any. However, that evening, a woman came to me in spirit form. I knew she wanted her soul healed. I didn't know what to do. I saw her soul as brilliant light and deep darkness. I thought maybe I should remove the dark, and yet, I hesitated and did nothing. She soon disappeared.

The next morning at the breakfast table, in front of all present, I told Cealo about the night visitor and my experience of thinking I should remove the dark. He adamantly said, 'Oh no, never take away the dark. Increase the light!'"[15]

---

14   *Messages from Jesus,* Third edition, p. 83.
15   *Messages from Jesus,* Third edition, p. 165.

I realized then that her darkness was partly karma, and by addressing her karma, she could increase the light within herself. Also, just as we send love-filled light into the world, I sent love-filled light to uplift her and help her address her karmic challenges.

Lord let your peaceful, gentle ray
Shine down on others strayed away.

———∞∞∞———

Our perception of opposition or contrast between fire and ice, acts of virtue and acts of vice, day and night causes us to experience them as dualities—hot and cold, good and evil, light and dark—instead of seeing them as aspects of The One, unified in oneness. Our lack of awareness of the unifying love and light of God has created this experience and, with it, the great dichotomy—the chasm between dualistic mortal consciousness and the blissful realm of God consciousness.

But when we begin to experience oneness through divine love and light and through meditation, we begin to see things from a non-dualistic perspective, as united in oneness, not as opposed to or sharply contrasted with each other. We realize that God is the One Source from which comes all we will ever experience, and our dualistic perceptions become subdued or vanish.

I know—not from intellectual knowledge but from divine experience and what Jesus has instilled in my heart—that everything is of God, the One who is many. I feel God in a flower, the food we eat, the people we meet, the trees, the air between us. Even our free will to choose unloving actions instead of loving ones is of God.

I experience God as oneness in brilliance seeing and in other aspects of wakeful meditation, a form of meditation that allows me to perform physical and mental activities while in the love and light of God consciousness.

In wakeful meditation, part of me sees each object as having its distinguishing characteristics and appearance, while at the same time another part of me sees all objects and actions in light and divine oneness.

Everyone has unique experiences of divine unity, their very own to hold dear. It may be for an instant, when a baby is born or when an aged person graces them with a hug. Other times this unity may be felt during meditation and its afterglow.

On earth, it is normal to experience opposition and contrast. Yet, I know a day will come when I will leave all this behind and be taken up, once again, in the oneness of God's infinite love and light. This is what happened to me when I visited "That Heaven".[16]

---

16   My visit to That Heaven is described in Chapter Ten.

THE BIBLE SPEAKS OF LIGHT:

"the Father of lights [God] with whom there is no variation or shadow. . . ."[17]

"And the light shineth in darkness, and the darkness comprehended it not."[18]

"That was the true light, which lighteth every man that cometh into the world." [19]

"God gives light both to the poor and the oppressor."[20]

"Be careful, lest the light in you be darkness."[21]

"Let your light so shine before men. . . ."[22]

"The Lord make his face to shine upon you, and be gracious to you. . . ."[23]

17 James 1:17
18 John 1:05
19 John 1:09
20 Proverbs 29:13
21 Luke 11:35, "
22 Matthew 5:16
23 Numbers 6: 25

Chapter Six

SPIRIT AND NATURE

"I only went out for a walk and
finally concluded
to stay out till sundown,
for going out, I found,
was really going in."

—John Muir

Today the forest surrounding our home has a lovely, ethereal impression of infinity. There is stillness, as if it is in awe of itself. The sun appears to be a ball of light vapor shining through the overcast sky, its spreading rays becoming increasingly diffused.

Crystalline rain is lightly kissing nature, settling like dewdrops upon the garden, while a rainbow peeks through the trees.

There is music in the wind as it plays amongst the swaying treetops. The near-hip-high, emerald bracken ferns, everywhere on the forest floor, are thirstily soaking up the rain. The chipmunks and squirrels drink from the handy flowerpot saucers, overflowing with water. Robins are bathing in the birdbath while hummingbirds hover with a flutter of wings amidst raindrops, sipping nectar from the multi-hued flowers in our garden.

Recently, there was a large, magnificent insect on the

outside of one of our sliding screen doors. He was beautiful and had long antennae, almost longer than his body. I studied him for a minute, then reached up and, with my index finger, touched him and, at the same time, in a teasing mood, said, "tickle, tickle, tickle", as I ran my finger lightly up and down his body, on my side of the screen. With that, he fell off and landed between the boards on the deck, catching himself by one of his front legs.

I stepped out the door and saw him hanging on for dear life. Imagining his hind legs trying desperately to catch some foothold, I realized he might be doomed to a state of imprisonment under the deck if he fell. I thought about pulling him up by his antennae, but I finally got a piece of paper, put it between the boards of the deck, brought it up under him, and was able to lift him out. He stood there for a moment. I think he was thanking me or telling me how upset he was, and then he flew away.

Our home is a retreat within a retreat. I feel as rich as I can be, for I love solitude and nature. I am at a point in my life where I mostly want to be alone in God, for there is an ever-deepening realization of God within me and in all things. Still, I know I don't have to isolate myself to have this realization.

I have often mentioned a pink angel in my books and have been aware of her since 1994, when my work as a healer began. It was as if she had always been there to help me. I always called her "My Pink Angel", for I had never been able to intuit her real name. When I would consider what it might be, my mortal mind would get in the way with fanciful names that I thought she must have, blocking my intuition.

It is through superconscious communion that she and I communicate. It is not like talking to one another; it is a knowing what each other is thinking. She has been with me for so long that when I have need of her, I just send out a thought for her presence, and she comes as if she were always there awaiting acknowledgement. In asking for her presence, there is never any shade of doubt that she will appear. I simply know she will come.

I often pass her on to others in need of her. When I worked in hospitals and nursing homes, sometimes I would ask patients if they would like my angel for the night and explain that she would wrap them in her wings and comfort them. No one ever refused her. Sometimes I would give her to several patients, one after another, knowing she was omnipresent.

On many occasions over the years, I too found comfort from her. When asked, she fans her wings over me to quiet my occasional sleepless nights or to comfort me.

I have seen her make herself so tiny she would fit in a pocket, or as big as a small house. Once she embraced a huge blaze and made it rain on a clear night to protect the surroundings. Another time, I gave her to a small boy to put in his pocket. His mother said that after that he refused to wear pants without pockets.

She is a beautiful angel, glowing in pink radiance, robed in layer upon layer of translucent gossamer, with wings of downy feathers.

I can always count on her, just as I can count on Jesus to be there for me. Each seems eager to serve when their help is needed. I believe my pink angel was given to me not only to help me, but to make it possible for others to receive comfort from her, knowing that an angel was helping them.

I often felt sad that I didn't know her name. It felt as though I were not paying due honor in calling her my "pink angel", for we all like to be called by our given names.

I finally decided to elicit her help and told her what I wanted to do. With pendulum in hand, I said I wanted to go through the alphabet one letter at a time and that she should cause the pendulum to move in a clockwise direction when I hit on the correct letter.

I started with "A". Immediately she indicated through the pendulum that her name started with an "A". I went through the alphabet and, when I came to "r", she indicated that was the next letter. Then came an "i", and an "e". I asked if she was the Archangel Ariel, and again it was positive for that!

I was elated! Finally I knew her name. "Ariel, Ariel, Ariel", I sang! I was so elated, I went out into the kitchen, where George sometimes sits at the dinner table editing my writings after I retire, and I said excitedly, "I know my pink angel's name!" Glowing with happiness for the revelation of her name, I could hardly contain myself!

I don't know much about angels, but I do know that the Archangel Ariel is well known. I had often thought of her name starting with the letter "A". There are different spellings, but it matters not. Finally, after all the many years of service that she had given me and so many others, I knew her name!

I searched the Web for more information and found that many consider her male, but some sources indicated that angels are neither male nor female. Archangel Ariel was always shades of pink to me, and I had been brought up to think that pink was feminine.

I read she is often associated with the earth. No wonder she could cause it to rain on a clear night.

Ariel is also credited with being a guardian/healer of animals, and she is often there when I am drawn to do healing work with animals.

I don't need to know everything about her, for my simple knowing continues to summon meaningful interventions, and nothing has changed between us, except now I can happily give Ariel credit where credit is due, addressing her by her given name.

"Bless your heart, Ariel, for your help and presence in our lives here on earth. I am so grateful for you. I love you."

<hr>

Sacredness exists in the midst of all life. I talk to nature and Spirit as I would to a friend, for I feel a conscious awareness of oneness with Spirit, animals, plants, storms, and all things that surround me. No doubt, this is because, in Spirit, all things are connected in oneness. There are no gradations of oneness, except in the human perception of oneness. God is everything that is, and nothing is outside of God.

Several years back, within the Retreat forest, I discovered three great white pine trees joined at the base. It is truly remarkable that they survived the lumbermen's clearing of white pines so long ago. They may very well be the highest trees on the Retreat.

I often stand with my back up against one or the other of them, and while looking far up into their height, I talk to them or release expressions of sorrow. Their energy is powerful and yet comforting. I have taken many people to experience the trees, sometimes leaving them there to unburden anxieties and stress and have a good cry.

These trees stand on a lot that was up for lease within our Clear Light Community. I had been concerned that someone would come along and cut them down to build a home. One day a friend, Dorothy, came to visit me and we went for a walk to see the trees. I expressed my concern for them, and she purchased a lease on the lot, to safeguard their presence.

And now a large maple tree just off our deck, which shades our house, has become diseased and weakened at the base. Wind could blow it onto our house and garage. Intuitively I have felt that it needs to be taken down. We have tried everything to save it, to no avail.

I have been talking to it and the trees surrounding it, to tell them it will be cut down in the next week. I have thanked the tree for its beauty, shade and presence in our lives. I have talked to the birds and animals that find shelter in its branches. It has been our companion, and we are saddened to see it go.

Several years ago, participants had gathered in the "wheelhouse" at the Retreat for my Healing Breath Retreat. We discovered very quickly that the room was inundated with hundreds of flies, most of them on the inside of the skylight, and they weren't able to escape.

I asked all the participants to open the sliding glass doors and other exit doors, then direct their thoughts, with respect, to the flies' guiding intelligence, requesting that the flies go out the exit doors, for they would die where they were. We did this for about five minutes with eyes closed, as we listened to the flies coming down from the skylight and finding their way out the doors. There was only a handful of flies left when we finished.

Every time I notice a fragrance from out of nowhere, I stop what I am doing and breathe in while looking around trying to see if there is an external source. Upon finding none, I realize it is from Spirit, and I breathe deeply to take it all in before it is gone. Sometimes it is a prelude to Jesus' presence. Most often, a kundalini rises within me with each breath, my pelvic floor clamps shut, and every pore is filled with the aroma, even my taste buds.

This tells me there is much to be discovered in creation beyond the physical realm.

> *There are more things*
> *in heaven and earth, Horatio,*
> *than are dreamt of*
> *in your philosophy.*
>
> —Shakespeare

As a child, my extended family went to my grandparents' farm every Sunday for a scrumptious chicken dinner.

Homemade bread, butter, noodles, pies, fresh veggies and fruit graced the big, oak, claw-footed dining room table.

My grandparents' farm was mostly fields of corn, potatoes, vegetables, fruit, cattle, a working horse, and free-roaming chickens. I loved the chickens. Usually I would chase them. It was great fun.

When I was about eight years old, the head honcho rooster decided his hens had had enough tormenting, and he started to chase me back up the hill to the farmhouse. I fell. And as I lay there screaming and trying to ward off this mad, foul fowl, he pecked me from end to end.

My grandfather heard my screams and came out the door on a run with an axe in his hand. He grabbed that rooster, threw him over a chopping block, and off went his head! But if that wasn't enough, the rooster got up and ran around the yard without his head! Later my grandmother cooked him up in a stew, which I did not eat.

My esteem for my grandfather and myself took a dive that day, for I didn't want to be someone who caused anything to die, not even a chicken. I felt really bad and never tormented the chickens again.

When we built our home here in the Retreat, I teasingly told members of the Clear Light Community board that I wanted free-roaming chickens. That didn't go over, so I tried to get the Retreat to put up a hen house in a section of their garden within the fencing. That didn't go over either.

I felt I knew something about chickens, because I had a booklet about how to raise chickens. Granted, the booklet was as old as I was, but it was a practical guide. I always packed my chicken book along with my other books and belongings when I made what I thought were going to be permanent moves.

When Cealo, a Buddhist monk, stayed with us, he told us about how he would go from village to village in Cambodia to distribute rice. He would call ahead to have the rice delivered to correspond with his visit.

In one village, a man and wife extended an invitation to provide Cealo shelter for the night. They told him they would be honored to serve him a meal the next day, and he accepted. He noticed that they had a rooster running around outside, but no other chickens.

The next morning, he did not hear the rooster crow. When the meal was served, he realized it was their one and only chicken. Without mentioning this, Cealo sat and ate the meal with them. But as soon as he could, he ordered a flock of chickens delivered to the couple.

I buy organic eggs direct from local friends who have chickens. One person has hens that lay green eggs. I think it is delightful when in my dozen eggs there are always a few green-shelled ones. I always save the green eggs for Sunday, just for the fun of it, or share them with guests when I serve them breakfast. Dr. Seuss knew what he was talking about in his *Green Eggs and Ham* book. I have sent money to *Heifer International*[24], choosing the option to send flocks of chickens to the poor. This empowers the recipient to have eggs and meat to eat, along with a means to earn income.

---

24   Heifer International is a non-profit organization whose goal is to help end world hunger and poverty through self-reliance & sustainability.

OUR ETERNAL SOURCE

O Spirit,
Thou art Infinite Glory.
All the earth is made in Thy image.
I bow to Thee.

What Thou hast fashioned
in the hills and fields,
in the earth and sky
bears Thy beauty.

May we treasure most
the works of Thine
and fashion ours
to fit Thy perfect plan.

May beauty reign,
may love prevail,
may goodness be
in all we think and do.

Thou art the Source
of every good,
the wellspring of
our fondest dreams;

and all we need
is found in Thee
and meant for us
eternally.

—George Johnston

Chapter Seven

SRF CONVOCATION

A grace bestowed—
words from God within me,
not through my floundering senses—
different in its essence
than conventional skill,
for it has warmth
and not the cold words of logic.

While I was writing *Messages from Jesus*—writings that are intensely personal and yet intended for others— Jesus mentioned a few topics that Yogananda would address with me in another book: meditation, awareness of God, and breath control.

I didn't give this much thought at the time, but later on, I wondered how I could possibly discuss such matters with Yogananda for a book. Yogananda had written extensively on these topics. What more could be said? Moreover, I did not have the personal bond with him that I have with Jesus. I continued to feel no urgency to write with him.

Jesus had said to me, *"You did not go to college to learn from just one teacher. You gathered knowledge through the experiences of many. Make room for other masters in your heart."*

My culture had taught me to regard Jesus and God as the only source of spiritual guidance, and after a life-long, personal relationship with Jesus, he was now urging me to open my heart to other masters.

I had already read Yogananda's book *Autobiography of a Yogi* and, after reading it a few more times, was stirred to read some of his other books and complete the Self-Realization Fellowship (SRF) lessons. His beautiful writings covered everything anyone would want to know about meditation and spiritual progress.

I was sensitive to the fact that Self-Realization Fellowship (SRF), founded by Yogananda, might frown on someone who would claim to be conversing with Yogananda and publishing what was said.

I felt little pressure to pursue a book with Yogananda, except from my dear husband, a devotee of Yogananda, who was anxiously waiting for me to establish an ongoing personal relationship with his guru, ask questions, as I had done with Jesus, and put our conversations in a book.

Even with Jesus' directive, deep down, I knew I had shut Yogananda out. As I write, Jesus, ever present, is conveying to me, "*You have veiled your heart to protect yourself from criticism because of what others might think. Where are you Brave Heart?*"

"I don't want to offend anyone."

"*Marvel at who you are. Cast open your courageous heart. There is nothing to fear.*"

With his words, I felt a revival of my unshrinking self from deep within.

I spent some time traveling in Michigan, Illinois and Arizona promoting *Messages from Jesus,* giving talks in bookstores, and homilies and workshops in Unity and other churches, and doing healing work and mentoring from my home. No advertising and no shingle out front; people just showed up. I provided healing workshops at Song of the Morning Retreat, where my husband and I live. It felt important to spread the messages in the book, which were given to me in conversations with Jesus and were intended for humanity. It kept me busy.

Many people asked, "Why do you think Jesus asked you to speak out?" My answer is, "Jesus wants to address the problems and opportunities of our modern world, which are very different from those of 2,000 years ago."

Truth has been elaborated upon and distorted by the sophistries of men down through the ages. In *Messages from Jesus,* Jesus dispels misconceptions and deepens our understanding of spiritual truth.

Eventually, I decided to start writing again. Not that I was ready for Yogananda to step forward. I just thought I would see where the writing would take me.

People had often asked me how I first came to have a personal relationship with Jesus. As some put it, "Why are you the way you are?" Thus, instead of writing a book with Yogananda, I found myself writing about my birth, my experiences with Jesus as a child, becoming a healer, and my life up to the time when I wrote *Messages.*

I knew I was still disregarding Yogananda. I did write of two brief encounters I had already had with him; one a reprimand and the other his beautiful presence. No dialogue took place.

I soon found out I was disregarding something else too. I thought I had the book (*Sustained by Faith*) finished until a friend of mine, while visiting in our home at the Retreat, asked to read it. Her words to me were frightful. She said, "You have left a whole big part of your life out of this book." I answered, "Yes," short and blunt. She said, "Tell me about it." I said, "I don't want to go there." She persisted with her questioning and, as I spoke of it to her, there were silent, horrific memories of abuse surfacing from out of the buried past as if I were being pelted with them. And from the little that I told her, she then said, "You need to write this, for it will help a lot of people." My heart sank.

What lay buried by my children and myself for over thirty years loomed before me begging for attention. I carefully began to address it and write. I prayed to Jesus to not leave me, for I was not sure I could tolerate reliving it. I had made myself a promise that I would never write of it. But I could see the merit of doing so for the benefit of those suffering abuse.

I had often felt a nudge, while immersed in meditation and in my writings, to pay some attention to and forgive the people and actions within the memories. By choosing to forgive, there was a letting go, a release, which gave me the power to heal. It took me another full year to complete *Sustained by Faith*. Of course, the book is about so much more than the few chapters on abuse. It's also about "a different way of being".

I have received many letters from people who tell me I

have written their story. I was and still am appalled by the number of people abused in our society. *Sustained by Faith* was meant to be written.

Then one day in 2006, I woke up with the intention to search out Yogananda. It was almost as if it were an urgency. I thought a good place to find him, or at least be in close proximity to him, would certainly be the SRF Convocation, held in Los Angeles every year. Surely I would come to know him better there. For some reason, I didn't consider that all I would need to do is to think of him for him to be here, as I often do with Jesus and Spirit.

In the air above Los Angeles, before landing, I had the feeling that I didn't want to be there and that this was a foolish quest. Coming from a quiet retreat and suddenly sensing the hectic world below threw me into anxiety. I simply wanted to be home. Wishing did not make it so.

Lingering pain from a knee replacement forced me to use the escalator, which was on the opposite side of the hotel from where the activities were taking place. I allowed extra time to get where I needed to go. Once I got in the big hall, I did breath work to decrease my pain and calm myself during group meditation. So much time would elapse while doing this that the meditation time would end just as I settled myself.

I was struggling with my physical self, as if in a tug of war. I kept wondering if I was supposed to be there. Was my ego, fearing its own demise, causing me to identify with my body, thus keeping me from new realizations? Nevertheless, in spite of my problems, I loved the talks by the monks and nuns, and listening to the chanting calmed me further.

My third day there, I took a bus tour to the SRF Lake Shrine. I wanted to meditate where Yogananda surely must have meditated. The premises are extraordinary. As a natural amphitheater, sloping land surrounds a small lake. Lovely statues, plantings, a windmill church, and a Gandhi World Peace Memorial encircle the lake, where a houseboat sits and swans glide to and fro. I walked slowly as I went around the lake, then I became concerned about missing the bus ride back to the Convocation, so I didn't take the time to go into the chapel. I thought of how disappointed in me my husband, George, would be, for I could not relax and feel Yogananda's presence. I sensed Jesus with me—within my heart. I prayed to Him for help. I still wanted to be home.

The next day, I took a bus to tour the Mother Center on Mount Washington, the international headquarters of Self-Realization Fellowship, where Yogananda lived, worked and meditated for many years. A newfound friend from Hawaii went with me. We had a restful drive through Los Angeles.

When the tour group got off the bus, I walked about ten steps, and suddenly, as if in a rush, Yogananda appeared in etheric form, walking toward me with open arms, welcoming me with a smile that is eternally engraved in my heart. Tears poured from my eyes as if they were a blessing, for there was no sorrow, only joy! I could sense people looking at me, yet I felt alone with him amongst the group.

Reality shifted into timelessness, as Yogananda and I walked together down the tree-lined boulevard. While my tears continued to flow, the periphery around us became softened by a bright mist. The ground I walked on became holy—silence prevailed. I found myself placing each of my steps slowly, carefully, meditatively, as if upon hallowed ground. Then, without warning, Yogananda was gone.

Still caught up in lingering slow motion, silence, and brilliance seeing, it was difficult to bring myself back to ground zero. I didn't want to. I stood for an eternal moment. Then I followed a tour group. I couldn't hear the guide in the abiding silence, so I gave up trying and, with a sudden sense of simply wanting to be alone, held back to do my own meditative tour.

As if Yogananda were watching out for me, he was at my side again. Tears of joy flowed once again, and I walked where he walked—past a water fountain holding a single lotus blossom closed in upon itself. I felt akin to the blossom, as if I too were closed up, restricted. We walked under a vine-covered pergola and sat in its shadow, on a bench. Through tears, I saw Yogananda smile at me. His brown/black eyes were merry. Warmth filled me. With everything still in haloed brightness and time without meaning, I became ever more oblivious to others.

His words were as a knowing, conveyed into my heart, mind and soul more clearly than if he had spoken audibly. He bowed his head as if it was an invitation to meditate. I thought I already was. Then losing all sense of body—in an expanded reality—I merged deeper into the silence.

Only after what seemed like a very long time did he bring my attention to the construction of the pergola and that . . .

"Things are not the same after one goes through the archway, for those who pass under it become introspective, pause to meditate and are changed."

He further conveyed, *"Meditation is a path to realizing one's God-self."* I filled with waves of bliss.

He pointed out the bark and leaves on various trees he had a hand in planting. I never expressed a word, spoken or unspoken. I simply swam in his presence.

> The moment you notice that
> you are just an instrument of God,
> the moment you become like a hollow flute,
> the wind will blow through you,
> and there will be music.
>
> —author unknown

Memories of his loving disciples and their work with him in planning and laying out the gardens and grounds, as well as things that were hidden from view—a quiet sanctuary set apart from the hectic world—were placed in my mind and heart. He smiled and filled my heart with a knowing that I would have loved being a part of it. He pointed out stepping-stones and the singing birds, and gave me imaginings of the view of the city at night. I wanted never to leave.

Then I looked over to my left, and there, within the fountain, the lotus blossom had opened to the warmth of the sun; and so had I, to the warmth of Yogananda.

I lost time . . . for suddenly I found myself on the front veranda of his home, alone and yet amongst many people, as if transported there. I stood still, with activity all around, simply knowing I was where I should be and whatever I should be doing would soon be pointed out.

As I stood rooted in my spot, in silence, a volunteer came

up to me and I found myself expressing to her, with words that seemed to come from outside of myself, that I wanted to go up to Yogananda's bedroom, but couldn't do the steps.

She motioned for me to follow her. Bypassing the long line of devotees extending from outdoors on the sidewalk and up the steps to the bedroom, she took me into Yogananda's elevator.

One step into the small elevator enclosure, and I felt the whole interior so filled with Yogananda's energy that tears of joy poured forth once again. The volunteer told me this often happens to others, and she would not let me get in line at the top of the stairs, taking me directly to Yogananda's bedroom. Momentarily, I felt unhappy to be singled out to go ahead of those waiting on the steps. But once inside, peaceful energy flowed through me like a breeze searching every part of me, and I was made calm amidst Yogananda's vibration, which permeates the room. From there, I went to the chapel and meditated without painful distraction, while still carrying his sweet presence within me.

A luncheon took place outside under a large, colorful canopy, and was delicious, what little I could eat of it. My hunger had vanished. I was about to leave the area when I suddenly found myself saying to the person sitting next to me, "I ask that you pray for our Song of the Morning Retreat. We are in need of direction." She said she would and asked if I would like a copy of Master Yogananda's prayer for praying for others. She was given the prayer at the Mother Center.

At this point, she took out a piece of paper and a pen and started writing. Once again, uncontrolled tears streamed down my face startling her as she wrote his words, for his presence was ingrained in them. This is what she wrote:

MASTER'S PRAYER FOR OTHERS

Grant_____'s heart's desire,

made legitimate

by your special grace.

Om Guru,

I love you.

Bless me.

After I returned home, I shared my experiences during the SRF Convocation with close friends. My time with Yogananda did not include dialogue. I never spoke; I never asked a question. He did not give me messages for others. It was a beautiful, personal welcome, with his words conveyed to me in heart talk. And partly because of that, I grew to love him—yet once again I set aside the thought of writing with him.

Chapter Eight

END TIMES

*"The enormity lies not only in the darkness
but in the worldwide, winning light
of those awakening in God."*

—Yogananda

Several months had passed after I returned from Convocation, when one evening as I lay in bed, I found myself asking Jesus, "I wonder why I don't call on Yogananda?"

In my heart I heard and felt Jesus' reply, *"Again I say, all beings in one are also within the Christ Consciousness. I am in you, and you are in me, and we are in the Father, the Son, and the Spirit, as one. Yogananda is within the Christ Consciousness. He is here in oneness."*

I thought of Yogananda, seemingly separate from me and yet omnipresent—his loving, silent presence more evident to me now since my visit to the Mother Center.

Yogananda and Jesus often manifest with a fragrance of roses—like a vapor floating in the air. Roses vary in appearance and fragrance, however, knowing they are roses we are often drawn to bow down to them in expectation of their lovely scent.

In my daily life, when I reflect on Jesus, I am often filled with His rose fragrance, even to the point of tasting it as it permeates into my very being. Since I cannot physically kneel, it is through my heart and soul—in single-minded devotion—that I give reverence, while envisioning myself bowing or prostrating before Him. Words cannot fully express the love I feel in doing this.

Jesus interrupted my thoughts, *"Yogananda said he would be able to be with everyone easier after he was gone than when he was in physical consciousness, and that you would find his whispers in your heart. Call his name."*

My experiences with Yogananda at the Mother Center left me with deep love for him. I could have stayed forever at the Mother Center. Every thought of him and every word of his I read or heard were as though they were hallowed. Still, I hesitated to call upon him.

Maybe my wavering to converse with Yogananda was because of the enormity of his presence and of the task, and my unfamiliarity with him. Moreover, he had already covered almost every aspect of meditation, spiritual living and God-realization in his writings, and I was content with the sweetness of my few experiences with him.

I found myself hesitatingly whispering, "Yogananda."

A warm, fragrant shakti energy filled me. I could hear my heart beat as blood coursed through my head in slow, strong waves. I could hear the familiar sound of a low drone, reverberating within my Self. I felt as though I were in a safe womb.

Then, Yogananda was before me, looking like he was enjoying himself; conveying his thoughts to me in the language of the soul, clearer and stronger than spoken word:

"Long before Convocation, I saw your devotion burst forth when you were told a certain 'Whispers from Eternity' book had been a personal copy of mine. At another time I watched your heart open when you heard that one of the harmoniums being used at the time had been mine, and later a lock of my hair stirred up deep memories within you. You could hardly contain yourself."

His words washed over me like rain. There seemed to be no breath in me, and I didn't care. The memories flashed before me, back to those separate instances, and I saw myself being overcome by his energy—his presence—in the objects back then, and with each object, each time, the very same words poured out from me, "Oh, can I just touch it!", and my hands became as if air as I gently laid them upon the book, harmonium and lock of hair.

I couldn't speak.

He continued, *"So it is understandable that you would feel overwhelmed with my presence, since you were overwhelmed with a mere book, harmonium and lock of hair!"*

I could feel Yogananda's amusement resonating within me, and I could feel the power and depth of his words. I saw his eyes sparkle in merriment. Energy flowed up my spine, as if it were playing strings on a harp. Feelings of blissful joy erupted within me. Laughter poured forth. I had no more control over it than I did with the gift of tears at the Mother Center.

"Whatever you are filled with you radiate."

I could barely contain myself. Laughter still bubbled

up as if it were releasing . . . I don't know what. I wanted to speak but couldn't find words. He interrupted my
thoughts.

*"Enjoy the moment. Think not of what is to come or has been.
I am with you. Just go within."*

I held my breath, as if breath was unimportant. Speechless
and smiling, I still couldn't think of words to say.

"Trust, lift that veil!" he seemingly bellowed loudly in an
accent remarkable to me, then sweetly he added, *"Sleep little
adept; go to sleep for now."*

I slept sound until two in the morning. And in my dreams
I heard Sri Yukteswar[25] saying those same words to me—*"my
little adept"*—while a recurring dream of being a young boy
in Sri Yukteswar's ashram came to me. And I remembered
my happiness while with him; sitting as close to him as I
could, listening to his wisdom day and night, and meditating.
All while some boys left the ashram because of his chastising
and demanding discipline.

Apparently, I still had things to get out of the way, for
once again, I set aside writing with Yogananda. Keeping this
blessed encounter close to my heart, I knew, when the time
was right, I could call on Yogananda and he would be there
for me.

---

25   Sri Yukteswar was Yogananda's guru. In *Autobiography of a Yogi*,
      Yogananda writes extensively about him, his teachings, and the strict train-
      ing he and other disciples received from him in their youth.

More time passed, then one day I found myself simply asking, as if he were present, "Yogananda, what do you want me to write about?" I hadn't even been thinking that I would be writing conversation with him, much less what I would be writing about. This simply spilled from my heart, as easily as if I were talking to Jesus.

He conveyed, *"Anything you want to."*

This surprised me. I tried to comprehend his response but didn't know how to reply at first. Thoughts kept crowding my mind.

It occurred to me that any philosophical writing in my books does not always come from me, but from Jesus and God, and sometimes George, for I am not that learned. I type the words given me, along with my own thoughts, but cannot always remember them later on.

Yogananda freed my concerns with whispers into my very soul, *"There are no demands on you to remember that which you have written. When moved to do so, read the words to others or share what you remember of the gifts which divine grace has given you, for you have a gift in the telling.*

"You are but a vessel, wherein wisdom—God consciousness— flows. Your vessel is never empty. You drink of it always, each time as if for the first time, and it refreshes you and is not bitter. You pour it upon others and it is pleasing. More words live in you, awaiting remembrance."

Quietly contemplating his words, I felt a wave of bliss, as if it were Yogananda himself flowing through my essence. I felt huge.

Ah, God's vastness did unfold,
all glowing like a dream,
Heaven manifest through my soul,
in endless, glorious sheen.

Oh, sweet God, resident in me,
with love I am made whole.
Open my heart that I might write
the words flowing through my soul.

Spirit of God unleash in me
living words with loving rays,
so those they reach, where'er they be,
may be divinely changed always.

Suddenly, as if urgency was needed, I could sense Yogananda becoming serious and thoughtful.

"There is too much focus on the fatalistic mind thought of some of humanity in regard to end times, which only serves to increase fear and negative energy on earth. Fear of the unknown often dulls common sense."

After thinking on this I said to Yogananda, "We seem to be witnessing the last of a civilization that may very well disappear under the bulldozers of unloving pursuit of wealth and power. Despite the assurances of our leaders, it appears that much of what is taking place globally is beyond their control."

Yogananda laid this in my heavy heart, *"Replacing the divinity of self with fear, a downward spiral ensues within the mind and actions of man. Global economics, advancing bacteria,*

infestations of insects, pestilence, environmental damage, wa-
ter scarcity, power grid failures, politics, famine, joblessness,
cyber-suppression, fear-mongers, terrorism, war, transitional
governments, and more, are troublesome and are a threat to
civilization.

"*I sense your concern for encroaching darkness. All the difficulties*
Mother Earth and its inhabitants are facing are penetrating every-
body's life. Side-by-side, the dark and the light are speeding up, with
chaos intensifying in parallel to an awakening in love and God."

"How can we prepare for such enormity?"

"*Set forth a plan for emergencies. Don't allow yourself to hold*
the consciousness of negativity, for it only adds darkness to your
environment and your soul.

"*Be loving today, so it becomes a loving past tomorrow. Thus*
consequences from mistakes will not be carried forth. Increase the
light with love for all, for the enormity lies not only in the darkness
but in the worldwide, winning light of those awakening in God.

"*You are not experiencing the end of Mother Earth, only*
change, for there has always been change. Mother Earth's natural,
cyclical changes—which often generate excessive wind, water and
fire conditions—along with man-made environmental disasters
evident in the warming of the earth and air pollution, are all a
part of earth's changes. Civilizations have come and gone, like the
cycles of creation, but God is forever.

"*Everything mankind does or says has an effect on the world.*
By casting a net filled with good intentions and pouring love and
light—as from out of a crescent moon—upon the world to pro-
mote love, health, harmony, peace, empowerment, and responsible

leadership for all, you will allow universal truth to shine its way into all hearts. Act on that thought.

"*You are blessed to be living through this vital time in history. The Clear Light Community you live in has the opportunity to be an epitome of 'World Brotherhood Colonies'—to live in harmony and love, to be self-sufficient, to give hope to others even in the midst of scarcity, suffering and uncertainties.*

"*Further, enlightenment lies within all people. When your life is full of God expression, you evolve upward with each incarnation, and in due course you will reach the final resting place in God.*"

I waited in stillness for more. There seemed to be no breath in me—cut off for an eternal moment.

Accustomed to the way things are
in the safe haven of sameness
—a place of refuge—
we avoid The Unavoidable
for as long as ever
and have need to return at life's end
to repeat, repeat the cycle.

How long, dear souls,
must you continue these roles
on the hub and spokes of the wheel
or the rim, the brim of demarcation
between God and self,
when just within reach
—in the still-point center of the hub—
The Unavoidable waits for you. . . .

A fleeting memory of when I was a very young child came to me. I had announced out loud, to no one in particular, "I want to be alive to see the end of the world!" I have no idea where that declaration came from. There was nothing to prompt it. It simply spilled out of my mouth, like a waterfall over a precipice.

If I had been older, I probably would have said "the end of this civilization," for I am certain my thoughts did not include the elimination of planet earth or the universe! The thought of "my world" ending was so profound to me at that age that I have never forgotten it.

I have a world map on the wall above my computer. I often use it to orient myself to where strife is in the world—to send love and light to those areas while praying for the good of all.

Suddenly, he spoke again,

"The rising and falling—creation and destruction— cyclically breathes, in due course, with the yugas, just as when a light goes out and another comes on. There is nothing to fear in birth or death.

"Those who do not allow darkness to reign in their hearts and do not lose sight of their divine essence and the spiritual nature of creation will experience higher and higher states of love and awareness. Many are climbing out of darkness, even amidst the chaos.

"Think of the finite dancing with The Infinite, freedom from fear, time embracing Eternity, and Mother Earth a paradise."

I took a breath, trying to clear my worrisome mind. I

asked Yogananda if there was a time frame for the end of our civilization. I received no answer to that question.

All this dialogue seemed fast and heavy. My mind swirled in a battle between so much information and peace.

I remembered what Jesus said in *Messages from Jesus*: "*I cannot predict the future; no one can. Predictions constantly change with prayer and love. Do not believe all the predictions that you hear. Only guesses and generalities can be made. Pray for peace. There is always hope. . . .*"[26]

Yogananda whispered into my heart: "*Little Mother, share your love with others, and rest easy now.*"

> Dancing edges of chaos and order
> —spiral fractals of Self—
> unable to light upon a straight line,
> the line of demarcation
> between God and duality.
> I surrendered. . . .
> All chaos disappeared,
> and I rested in God.

Yogananda's comments were in 2010, and now, early in 2011, as I go over the book prior to publication, the world is witness to Japan's massive earthquake and tsunami, followed by widespread destruction, nuclear disaster, and great misery.

Elsewhere there have been fires, drought, floods, mudslides, fierce storms, wars, hardship, and revolutions. I am

---

26   *Messages from Jesus,* Third edition, p. 113.

sure, at this time of upheaval and change, many are praying with heavy hearts for those in our world who are suffering.

In the midst of destruction and suffering around the world, I see the poor helping the poor, strangers helping strangers, international rescuers coming to aid those in need, and countries helping countries.

Out of the rubble of a disaster, one sees light in the compassionate hearts of men and women. On television I saw a dog who, though capable of leaving a flooded area, stayed to watch over another injured dog. Even animals can show compassion.

Chapter Nine

BREATH PLAY

The evening floods the space.
With quiet thoughts,
I spend my time alone
in all the splendor here.

B reath control was a topic that Jesus had told me
Yogananda would share with me. [27] But I had put it into
the recesses of my mind.

Then . . .

Early one morning, I became aware of Yogananda's presence, while at the same time, a suggestion that was almost
musical permeated my heart: *"Share what you know about
breath control, which was instilled within you lifetimes ago."*

Suddenly, a wave of inadequacy came over me. I felt that
what I knew was little, compared to his expansive teachings,
for controlling my breath was a rather simple practice that I
grew up with.

Then words spilled out from me, "I don't like to refer to it
as breath control, for it is more like play."

With that he laughed loudly and with a booming voice
said, *"Blessed are you who recognize that which God teaches aside
from strict ritual."*

---

27   *Messages from Jesus,* Third edition, p. 202.

Reading my awestruck mind and with a grin, Yogananda said, "*Go with the knowing.*"

———∞∞∞———

A few years ago, I wrote a booklet about using breath control for healing, based on my personal approach to it and what I had learned from others about its benefits.

I use my booklet, *The Healing Breath,* as class material at Healing Breath workshops and silent retreats at Song of the Morning. I felt that the booklet was divinely inspired, that Jesus and maybe Yogananda had a hand in it. But I can't be sure.

I give it to you here, in an effort to present as an effortless practice, what some think is complex. For often things are simpler than we think they are.

Even the lightest, subtlest intended breath heals. What wonder the quiet mind and the brush of breath!

The Healing Breath exercise expands and channels the life force within you for healing yourself and others.

Breathing is much more than simply oxygenating and purifying blood by moving air in and out of the lungs. The breath is a vehicle for moving subtle energies, referred to in the spiritual teachings of India as *prana*, or life force.

The Healing Breath is a form of Pranayama—breathing performed with the specific intention of controlling life force. Pranayama can also be thought of as the breath of the living universe.

The word "pranayama" is comprised of two roots: "prana" and "yama".

"Prana" signifies vital energy, or life force, which permeates the universe at all levels and permeates and enlivens one's body.

"Yama" means control and, in the usual meaning of the word "pranayama", refers to controlling the life force through concentration and intentional breath control.

By practicing the Healing Breath exercise with dedication and the right attitude, you will begin to notice in a short amount of time—days or weeks—subtle, positive changes in your demeanor. The Healing Breath, as well as many other forms of pranayama, has the potential to:

- calm the mind and body,

- help clear the mind before meditation,

- relieve stress-related disorders,

- improve autonomic functions, for example, digestion and elimination,

- bring temporary or lasting relief from pain,

- rejuvenate the nervous system, endocrine glands, bodily tissues, cells, and organs,

- remove toxins from your body,

- extend life,

- enhance perception,

- steady your mind and strengthen your will,

- enable you to withdraw your attention from the physical world during meditation,

- fill you with light and bliss.

Almost anyone can practice the Healing Breath exercise, for it requires no special knowledge or skill and can be done anywhere, anytime. However we waste our time if we practice it without a positive attitude for success.

PRECAUTIONS

If there is a physical condition affecting one's cardiopulmonary system, a doctor should be consulted before attempting the exercise. In addition, please keep in mind that breathing is an automatic process, controlled by the autonomic nervous system. Normally, one does not have conscious control over it, and if one tries to forcibly control it, one may be working against the body's needs.

Therefore caution should be used. Always do what comes naturally, without force, when working with your breathing pattern. If you begin to feel dizzy, you may need to breathe more slowly or stop the Healing Breath exercise.

EFFECTS from the Healing Breath

Our integrated physiological, psychological, and spiritual make-up is affected by changes in any part of it. Change in one part of our system affects every other part. Our physical, mental and spiritual state is affected by our breathing, and our breathing is affected by our physical, mental and spiritual state.

Physical effects

Regular practice of the Healing Breath brings beneficial

change to every part of our body-mind-spirit. As the mind is quieted by the slow breathing exercise, the brain and glands become better able to regulate chemicals that, in turn, regulate our biochemistry: we sleep more soundly, our overall mood improves, we are better able to have deep meditations, and we become less anxious.

In addition, muscles relax, pain is decreased, the cardiovascular and pulmonary systems become stronger and healthier, physical endurance and stamina increase, digestion improves, and mental capacity for concentration and problem solving are enhanced.

Addiction to smoking (or other drugs) or cravings of any kind may be diffused and eventually eliminated if the Healing Breath is done properly and regularly.

Psychological effects

Our psychological make-up leans on our self-created ego. When the ego is agitated or threatened, we may also become agitated and lose our focus. Then the breath becomes quick and shallow. The process of trying to suppress the ego may create this agitation in us because we are threatening our ego with the possibility of extinction—something the ego fights against fiercely. The ego is vying for control over you and tries to keep you engaged in the world of duality. This may be experienced as a busy mind during meditation.

Thus, in initiating practice of the Healing Breath exercise, we command the ego to leave, and we must be aware that the ego may defend its status by causing us to doubt or feel anxious or restless. We must be prepared to overcome the ego's false concepts with the power of truth and inner calm.

Prior to working with a healing client, I adamantly address my ego by saying, "Okay ego, get out of here, be gone." Only then can I "let go and let God", and healings occur. If we give in to the ego's desire to interfere, we give up control over our lives and stay quagmired in the confines of the ego's false domain.

Our freedom to choose what we know is best for us is the only power the ego cannot withstand, and as our breath becomes longer and deeper, we find ourselves in a peaceful, relaxed state of consciousness. With continued practice, a new understanding arises that can identify and extinguish any unwanted mood with negligible effort.

Spiritual effects

We are all spiritual beings by nature, so in reality, there is nothing spiritual to be gained from practicing the Healing Breath that we don't already innately have. What we are really doing is becoming more aware of our native spiritual state.

With regular practice of the Healing Breath exercise, the distractions of form, sound, smell, taste, touch and thought disappear, and we can calm the busy mind and relax the body, heal ourselves and others, and gain a conscious realization of our pure, non-dualistic nature as spirit. Then we realize that all is one in Divine Love . . . in God.

OPTIONAL:

Prior to practicing the Healing Breath, you may wish to perform hatha yoga and/or clear your aura to remove negative energies so they do not manifest in the mind as negative thinking or in the body as a physical problem.

You can clear your aura by feeling the differences in the "air" around you. Start by stating an intention to clear your aura, then, with your hands above your head, slowly and gently bring them down through the energy field that surrounds your body. Feel with your hands, letting them slowly move guided by intuition, while evaluating the differences in the air around you.

Some feelings you may sense are heaviness, warmth, cold, negativities, smoothness, etc. This is your aura, or energy field.

Over and over, bring your hands through the aura. If you intuitively feel like grasping something you want to get rid of, do so, then toss it gently away from you, or brush it down and away from you, asking God to take it where it will do no harm.

End when you feel intuitively that you are clear.

BREATH PATTERN

Normal breathing is performed in the following pattern:

1. inhalation
2. retention (holding the breath in)
3. exhalation
4. retention (holding the breath out)

Normally, a retention lasts only for a moment after each inhalation and exhalation.

However, if one fixes the mind steadily on the inhaled energy (life force) spreading within the body, the retention will naturally be extended to longer and longer periods of time.

BASIC HEALING BREATH

Set an intention to activate the Healing Breath.

Tell the ego to leave, then give it no more attention.

Say a prayer to be filled with God's healing energy.

Quiet yourself. Be comfortable. Close your eyes.

Take a deep breath, sigh it out. Drop your shoulders.

Focus on your normal rhythmic breathing through your nose, for a while. Calm your mind. Should you find yourself thinking about something other than your breath, withdraw your consciousness from those thoughts and calmly return to watching your breath flow.

Arjuna says in the Bhagavad Gita (6.34):

"O Krishna, the mind of man is restless, rash, tumultuous, willful and strong. I consider it as difficult to tame the mind of man as stay the wayward wind."

Then Krishna goes on to say (6.35):

"Certainly, the mind is hard to restrain and wavering, but by self-discipline and yoga practice, the mind may be controlled."

Focusing on your breath helps to still the mind. Relax and breathe in deeply. Fill your belly and expand the air into your ribs and chest during each inhalation, then during each exhalation, let the abdomen come in. This is the healthiest form of breathing we can do. Babies do it. We do it automatically when completely relaxed.

Listen to the sound of your breathing.

Feel your breath as it enters and exits your body.

When moved to do so, breathe in, hold, and sense the breath as energy filling the whole body. Each tiny cell seems to fill with this prana, bathing in healing light as you hold the breath in a state of rest, not forcing it to stay.

Exhale very slowly and gently; relax. There is a sense of patience, as this is a pleasant sensation of exhalation.

Repeat until you feel you are finished.

End with a Thank You to Spirit.

OPTIONAL:

You may wish to direct the breath as energy to each chakra, in turn. This helps to open these centers in a profound way. The chakras bring heightened spiritual awareness when one's energy, instead of flowing outward into the sense organs, is directed into these centers in the brain and spine.

HEALING BREATH FOR SPECIFIC PURPOSES

Continue on from Basic Healing Breath, as follows:

As you breathe in, scan your body for any discomfort or pain, or your mind for any negative emotion that needs healing.

As you hold the healing breath, send it into a specific area and let it linger there. Or ask God to send the healing breath where you need it, if this is not evident to you.

Breathe out. Relax. Slowly release tension and pain—make any discomfort comfortable.

Again, breathe in. Send energy to the part of the body or mind that needs healing and let it linger there, or just let the energy flow where God sends it.

Breathe the healing breath out from that area. Push the problem or pain out.

Or exhale slowly through the nose or mouth, feeling or imagining the breath taking the problem with it.

Repeat until you feel you are finished.

Move on to another painful area or emotional or spiritual problem that might need healing.

End with a Thank You to Spirit.

This is a healing treatment on all levels. It brings a blissful, peaceful state. It purifies, nourishes and strengthens us emotionally and spiritually, as well as physically, by the increased energy (light) that flows from the practice of this technique.

HEALING BREATH FOR HEALING OTHERS

Continue from Basic Healing Breath, as follows:

Visualize a person or situation. Set an intention that healing occur for their highest good.

Breathe in and hold the healing breath comfortably, exhale, hold. Repeat.

As you do this, feel your breath slowing down and energy building within.

With each slow intake of breath, fill your heart or your upraised hands with healing energy.

Slowly release the energy by breathing out your heart or hands toward the person or situation, for healing. They do not have to be present.

See the person or situation healed.

Continue until you feel you are finished.

End with a Thank You to Spirit.

If you are able to practice the Healing Breath easily, without discomfort or difficulty, it will be of great benefit to you and others. It can be used to bring about an overall improvement in well-being, as well as to address specific ailments. It can be used for self-healing or healing others at any distance.

The Healing Breath exercise is easy to master if you take time each day to practice it. Jesus often said to me, "*Practice, practice, practice.*"

Practice without struggle and be patient. It may require several months for you to be able to feel energy filling parts of your body. I use these techniques the instant I awaken in the morning and before bedtime to clear and heal myself and to help alleviate any pain, but they can be done anytime, anywhere.

The Healing Breath is not only an excellent place to begin a spiritual practice, but it is an excellent place to return to for those who have spent many years practicing a variety of spiritual techniques without significant progress. Even adepts use breath work to begin their meditation practice, for they know it will quickly bring body, mind, and spirit into balance and prepare the way for entering deep states of meditation. I use it for self-healing and to quiet my mind before meditation.

Until full command of the breath is accomplished, it is very difficult to go deep in meditation, and you may become frustrated in your efforts and disillusioned with your path.

Jesus, ever near, *"Even so, in your practice, be assured that you are changing within in subtle ways you may not be aware of. You may be more intuitive, more self-assured, more patient, happier, and more aware of God's presence in your life."*

The Basic Healing Breath exercise is the breath play I have practiced since I was very young. I did not think of it as healing until many years later. I only knew that I felt wonderfully peaceful within. I also did not know I was aura clearing as a child when I brushed the pain from a scrape or stomachache, or calmed myself before a test or when upset.

Yogananda, also near, lit up with a smile, *"I love how you call this uniting in God 'breath play'! There is ever more that breath gives rise to, as you know, just waiting in the wings for sincere seekers of truth."*

—ↀↀↀ—

We did not enter this physical experience to suffer, but rather to expand in the joy of unfettered creativity in harmony with the will of God, and to have *"experiences of God in the beauty, life, and the intelligence of nature as one."*[28]

Humans originally were on earth in a high state of consciousness, aware of their oneness with each other, all of creation, and God. In the Bible, this blissful existence was symbolized as the Garden of Eden. *"Then mankind began to be influenced by dualities within the earth plane and, instead of remembering the oneness of pain, pleasure, joy and all there is, mankind accepted pain and suffering as separate. This inability to be at one with all aspects of creation led to a perceived separation from, and diminished ability to commune with, The Divine. And the chasm grew ever wider."*[29]

Pain had a purpose and was intended to warn us of actions and influences that could damage the body. By judging pain as separate instead of experiencing it as unified in oneness with all that is, we diminished our awareness of oneness, our awareness of God, and began to perceive ourselves as separate from God. Not feeling our complete unity with God, we began to identify, instead, with our limited physical body, and our perception of pain became intensified.

28 *Messages from Jesus,* Third edition, p. 166.
29 *Messages from Jesus,* Third edition, p. 166.

In his writings, Yogananda said that we intensify our perception of pain through fear, imagination, and identification with the body. From what Jesus and Yogananda have said, I can only conclude that pain, the way it is felt by most of us in our present state of consciousness, is unnatural—far different from the experience God originally created as a warning for us—and even though pain still serves a purpose, we should try to alleviate it, as well as eliminate the actions that cause it.

I give thanks to my body, which appears to encase my soul here on earth. I am aware of its limitations as mine for a time. I am mindful of the oneness of God in all of creation, even in me as an integrated whole—body, mind, and soul. For God is within all things as they are, and nothing is outside of God. Even so I will leave behind the body and mortal mind when God takes me home.

Jesus came as if he were listening:

"I have watched so many of you relight the memory of oneness until it becomes easier and easier, and you remember that, that which gives you joy or pain has already been absorbed into oneness in God."

"My Beloved Jesus, you come to me as easy as a floating feather falling from out of the sky. I love you. I am honored by your presence in my life, and I thank you for your help in fulfilling my life's purpose."

BREATH PLAY

The evening floods the space.
With quiet thoughts,
I spend my time alone
in all the splendor here.

The breath of God is felt
upon my brow.
I gasp, and hold;
Eternity comes . . . is spent.
Then I let the vapor go.

Within the peaceful bliss,
the breath comes once again.
As swift as I can feel its love
I send it out to you, my friend.

Chapter Ten

I HAVE BEEN IN THAT HEAVEN

The glory of God in Oneness reigns
throughout the seen and unseen worlds.
It shines most bright in one part
and less in others.

I have been in that heaven
wherein He shines most bright,
and flowed in endless love,
before my return.

With words not graced enough,
and memory that cannot hold the
magnitude of glory I beheld,
I strive to tell of it.

What I remember of that heaven
—God's Holy Kingdom shining in my soul—
is now the subject of my singing. [30]

---

30   Adapted by Mary Ann Johnston from Dante's *The Divine Comedy*,
Paradiso, Canto 1:1-7.

My beliefs do not come from theological doctrines. They arise from an inner knowing and from Jesus' presence in my life. Jesus taught me truths about God that superseded teachings I learned in my church. Even as an innocent, unquestioning child—no matter what I was told—I knew I would go to God in the hereafter, not to departed relatives. This knowing was deep within me, not a conclusion I had come to by thinking about it. It just was, and still is.

In *Messages,* speaking to Jesus, I wrote, "I once looked closely into my bathroom mirror at my face. Nose to nose. I asked myself in the mirror, 'Who are you?' Again, adamantly, I asked, 'Who are you?' Face after face quickly flashed before me, one right after the other. Just like those instances on television where they flash view after view, faster and faster. I saw old people, young, every color and nationality. The no-noise was deafening. I stayed with it as long as I dared. It was hard to tear myself away—physically and emotionally hard. The experience was so profound that I finally gasped at the totality of it. It was frightening. With difficulty, I physically had to push myself back, as if from a suction. What was this hold on me?"

And Jesus answered:

"These people were your past lives, and in acknowledging them, they showed themselves to you, and you were drawn even further and further into the past. You have lived for eons. Enlightenment is ongoing for you. Your channels are fully opened. You have no bad karma. You can go to God any time you wish."[31]

---

31   *Messages from Jesus,* Third edition, pp. 186-187.

My soul has had many opportunities, through reincarnation, to grow in wisdom and love toward fulfilling its longing for final absorption into God. It is this way for all of us, often unaware.

Song of the Morning has a teen week every summer. One of their activities is to come to our home in the Clear Light Community, across the river from the Retreat. For the past four years, about twenty teens and their counselors would gather on our deck and out onto the lawn to listen to me speak of what I know of healing, an introduction for many of them.

When they came in the summer of 2005, the birds were singing, the trees were swaying in a gentle wind, and the sun shone down from a clear blue sky, as they gathered once again on our deck and lawn. A hush filled the air, quieting all of us. My granddaughters, Jackie and Allysha, were among them. I gave Jackie a stone to hold to take her mind off her problems, for she was struggling with some issues.

I began to speak to them about giving and receiving healing, the wonders of nature, and God. I talked of energy and how to sense or feel it. I spoke of communicating with nature and being receptive to nature's responses. I spoke of the all-inclusiveness of oneness.

Well into my talk, I placed my hands upon my heart, feeling within, a shift—pain radiating across the central part of my body under my breasts and ribs ... a heart attack! I knew what it was—just as night knows the coming of dawn—but chose not to own it, not to acknowledge it, for I did not want to frighten the children.

Suddenly, through no effort of my own, my subject turned from healing to bravery, and I was filled with what to say, for I had never lectured about bravery in the past. I wanted to tell them what was important, before they left ... or I left.

The words simply came to tell them how it takes bravery to confront, with love, the difficulties and problems they and others around them are experiencing in the world today; and wisdom to recognize God's presence while doing so.

As the radiating pain continued, I spoke of future challenges and that one should always strive to do what is right and true, with intelligence, grace, and above all, love.

I was in peace,
under an umbrella of Spirit,
transfixed on my task.
With no sign of concern,
I sat on the brink
and talked on and on
to the listening children. . . .

I wanted to sing the Gayatri mantra for them and prayed that I could complete it. I explained, "The Gayatri mantra is a sacred, Sanskrit prayer to God as the Source of light. When I sing it, I feel God's love filling me—to give to you—and even after loving you fully, I can love all others with the same equal intensity, for God's love is never diminished."

The Gayatri is my favorite mantra. I sing it to the forest, our garden, and all of nature. I sing it for the world. I often sing it silently, for I find that the silent singing fills my mind and leaves no room for thinking about other things—things that take my focus away from God. Before I sang, I asked them to imagine:

> Imagine . . . imagine . . .
> with each breath,
> loving warmth filling you—
> as if you were a vessel to be filled. . . .
> Light surrounds you. . . .
> Love fills you . . . to overflowing.
> Then, in a moment you choose,
> throw open your arms and,
> as a gentle shower,
> rain forth love and light over the earth,
> over friend or foe or situation.

Thus, I showed the children how they could send abundant light and love over all the earth or to those in need, and also explained that we shine brighter in response to our loving intentions.

Then I sang the Gayatri:

> *Om . . . Bhur Bhuva Svaha . . .*
> *Om . . . Tat Savitur Varenyam . . .*
> *Bhargo Devasya Dheemahi . . .*
> *Dhiyo Yonah Prachodayat. . . .*

Peace settled over us. There wasn't a sound from the teens for a time. Then the visit was over.

As they were leaving, I took time to counsel a girl who came into the house, and also gave some advice to a counselor who sought my thoughts on a problem he was having. Someone handed me a rock and another a flower. It was only after everyone was gone that I finally told George he needed to get me to the hospital, for I was having a heart attack.

Ten minutes after arriving in the emergency room, the doctor verified that I was indeed having a heart attack. I suddenly felt faint, and my heart stopped. I thought "Jesus, Jesus, Jesus". Without a beat in my heart, I left my ego behind and my soul departed from my mortal shell and entered God's holy kingdom.

I have no gift to remember the whole of it, nor words to describe what I felt and saw that lies deep within my consciousness. For except in a limited and imperfect way, my words and metaphors are not adorned enough to depict the glory of God and God's supernal realm. It is through the memory of it in my soul that I often experience the feelings, silence, light, and love of That Heaven.

There was no Saint Peter at a gate, no divine being sitting on a throne, no life experiences passing by me, no tunnel, no angels, no dearly departed, just an instantaneous merging into union in God, in peace, silence and beautiful, pastel-colored dancing rays, like an indescribable aurora borealis.

My soul was caught up in this endless God—who had no form, nor body—flowing in streams of light, as bright as a thousand, thousand suns, but as soft as moonlight. I was one with all, indistinguishable from God as light and love.

There was no sense of time . . . time was meaningless. No landmarks or sense of place, but I knew I was in God. No sense of body, no form, no burdens, no sorrow, no sound of any kind; these were all left behind. No ego, no desire, no questions, no fear, no judgment, no sense of separation.

I was simply in God . . . in all-encompassing love and light.

Oh . . . the joyful realization
of knowing such a passing is open to all,
for everyone on their final journey to God,
where mind is non-attached to duality,
unfettered by ego,
with no desires nor residues of diversion,
nothing to regard and nothing to release,
nothing to believe, nothing to doubt,
nothing to judge,
nothing to lose,
and love is awarded rest in God.
Flowing unbounded, for a timeless eternity
—being, just being—
on the other side of delusion,
where boredom with its brazen mask can never be,
as if asleep, but wide-awake,
at one with the flowing lights of souls,
at peace in oness with God.
Suddenly, I leave the bliss . . .
I'd not made the choice . . .
back into the chaos of duality,
back into the realm of breath.
Yet calmness persists.
God lives in me, and I live in God,
even in the midst of life,
and I go on.

I have no memory of why I might have returned. Breath linked my soul with my mind and body and I was instantly thrown into the dichotomies and dualities of earth—still carrying a trace of heaven in my memory, which induced in me a profound longing, like a divine, magnetic pull, to return to God. I was devastated, to say the least.

Oh . . . let me take wing to the endless heaven.
Let me rise on the breath of God
and soar as waves of aurora
amongst eternal rays in God.

I was transferred to a hospital in Petoskey, Michigan, and family rushed to my bedside. The memory of God in the afterlife held me in such intense longing that my words and actions caused George and other family members to worry, for I so longed for God that, even in my quiet state, I spoke of suicide in my desire to return to God. Both the longing and re-adapting to the physical world were intensely painful.

Suicidal thoughts were quickly replaced when Jesus abruptly reminded me of what He said in *Messages from Jesus* about those who commit suicide, *"They reincarnate to work off that karma."*[32]

Suicide was definitely not a shortcut to God! Thus, I was reminded that, if I were to purposely destroy my body through suicide, I would reincarnate to balance the karma, and eventually resume the process of remembering God. I would not be able to go straight to that heaven.

My two, teen-aged granddaughters came around the

---

32   *Messages from Jesus*, Third edition, p.277

curtain at the foot of my hospital bed and simultaneously both started sobbing and crying loudly. Their outburst catapulted me abruptly back to ground zero, shaking me from thoughts of suicide, leaving me grounded by their love.

I put forth an effort to survive and was able to bring to the light my soul's knowing that I truly must stay the course, no matter how difficult, for living on held the promise of an infinite God-presence awaiting me when this life is over.

Still, I grieved, as I so longed for what had been lost. For I was never so blessed as I was then. There are no words that fully convey what I experienced. Even though I try, poetic language does it no justice. And what the soul felt and saw, the mortal mind cannot wholly contain. I frequently get teased with a touch of that heaven followed by momentary feelings of unquenched longing for divine communion—agony and ecstasy all rolled into one.

Ah, what a selfish, foolish wish it was to think I could simply go to heaven and sidestep my work before its completion. I now know the reward for finishing my work far outweighs any trial that might be ahead for me. And even when my work is done, I will be patient until the appointed time when I am fully taken up in God.

Chapter Eleven

LONGING

Oh Infinite God, listen to my plea.
Illuminate my memory of that heaven
shrouded by my mortal mind.

In the silence of meditation, I sometimes lose awareness of my body, as if I were an observer without a body.
However, even though I intermittently bask in such meditations and long to return there, they have never given rise to
the depth of longing for God that came when I returned
from heaven after dying. I believe the magnitude of longing
for what I experience in meditation is not as intense because,
in meditation, the ego still lingers near and keeps me from
experiencing absolute oneness with God.

George reminded me to read what I wrote in my book
Sustained by Faith, of an experience of heaven that Jesus
showed me some time ago.

Next, a glimpse of "Heaven" came before me, another unstained garden . . . of paradise promised. It was flowing
with all colors and no colors, all movement and no movement. There was no physicality nor fixed shapes or forms.
The peace was beyond imagining, and it is only through
the mind of my soul that I can do any justice in the telling
of this, for my physical body was not present there.[33]

---

33   *Sustained by Faith*, p. 158

It is amazing to me that I forgot this vision, which Jesus led me through. It parallels what I experienced in my death, except that in this vision my ego was still with me. I was the "observer" getting a taste of heaven, not totally merged into it, so there was still a sense of separation from God.

In my death, however, I was no longer an observer. The ego was gone and I was freed from the ego's fundamental illusion—separation. Thus I became fully aware of my oneness with The Infinite.

> Ah, the vastness of my temple,
> Made known to me upon a time,
> Heaven's place within my soul,
> Where endless glories shine.
>
> In the light that set me free,
> Graced with joy and song,
> My clinging ego flowed from me:
> I went where I belong.
>
> Only departed could I be free.
> In the Oneness I was whole.
> I had no body I could see;
> I saw God through my soul.
>
> Spirit of God, in Oneness reigns,
> Flowing in endless rays,
> Filled with love and peace and light,
> I will remember all my days.

Jesus said to me in the past, "*Since God is everywhere and*

God is in heaven, you must realize this highest heaven is a state of consciousness. Heaven is not a place in time. Truly I say unto you, thou shalt dwell in the house of the Lord when you become Self-realized, without the limitations of the ego, even while embracing life on earth or in the astral or causal plane."[34]

From Jesus' teachings in *Messages from Jesus*, we learn that, long ago, humans created the ego by making comparisons, judging pleasure as good and pain as bad. By judging, we cut ourselves off from awareness of the inseparability (oneness) of all things, and we began to see division instead of unity.

"This inability to be at one with all aspects of creation led to a perceived separation from, and diminished ability to commune with, The Divine."[35]

We lost conscious awareness of our oneness with God and creation, and instead of identifying with the light and love of God within us (the Self), we identified with our limited, finite, mortal body and came to believe that we are separate from everything that exists outside of it.

The ego is rooted in the false idea that we are separate from the One Spirit within us and within all things, and blinds us to the truth that we are integral aspects of the whole. It is the "fallen mind", always fighting for its own survival by causing us to doubt truth and to look for happiness in physical pleasure rather than in divine pursuits. Its network of delusive thoughts and negative feelings creates a state of consciousness in which our awareness of our blissful, loving, spiritual essence (the Self) and our unity with God is blocked by false

34 *Messages from Jesus,* Third edition, p.271.
35 *Messages from Jesus,* Third edition, p. 166.

identities, worldly attachments, strong aversions, deep-seated fears, greed, guilt, condemnation, hatred, arrogance, anger and many other destructive and limiting thoughts and feelings. All of us have recognized these thoughts and feelings in others, but we don't always recognize them in ourselves.

Because of the ego, we often feel a deep sense of incompletion and are always searching for happiness outside of ourselves. The infinite love, bliss, and glory of our omnipresent Self and God are almost completely veiled and invisible to us. The only way to find completion is to awaken from the influence of the ego.

In observing my own actions and reactions, it seems as if transforming into an egoless person is taking too long. Sometimes my ego gains the upper hand—fearful of extinction—and turns my sweetness into anger, worry and fear about worldly and personal matters, which only further feeds the ego. The ego clings as if it had tentacles.

When my ego comes to the fore, I often get an uncomfortable feeling of imbalance in myself, which triggers remembrance that I am a child of God, physically expressing on earth and one with all creation. Then, I can perceive perfection within my imperfection and see God expressed in everything.

Through unconditional love, positive thinking, and by opening to the inflow of divine grace, guidance and intuition, the ego may be purified and eventually transcended. As its more gross aspects, such as hatred, greed and arrogance, are overcome, one begins to work on its more subtle aspects, for example, being overly critical of others, thinking of oneself as better than others, and the belief that we are separate from the light, love and oneness of God.

Belief in separation, instead of awareness of unity, is the fundamental illusion upon which all the other thoughts, feelings and illusions of the ego depend. They, in turn, support this belief.

At this time in history, it is crucial to be loving and forgiving, and more aware of the oneness of everything. We praise good and condemn evil, but if we make a practice of mentally judging and condemning those who commit crimes or disagree with us, we are unable to feel love and oneness with them and let go of the ego's belief in separation.

By simply embracing the possibility that there is a single Source of all that is, we have opened the door to healing the illusion of separation. We have opened the door to healing the dualistic way of thinking that arises when we judge and condemn things and people, and separate them into categories of good and evil. Instead of judging and condemning, we should try to know the Spirit that underlies and connects all things and people, and seek to understand the purpose behind the cosmic drama set in motion by God.

Often, shedding the limitations of my mortal self, seemingly through no effort of my own, I am teased by fleeting, overwhelming reenactments of the egoless, ecstasy-filled peace of my immersion into heaven, and the unquenched longing I experience afterward is like a powerful magnet, so intense it is almost painful.

I was not bound to mortal existence in any way in my visit to that heaven. There was no ego. Not bound to ego, I was truly free.

LONGING

There, amidst the sweet and sour of my dream,
if only for a moment of peace,
a breath of selflessness comes, then goes. . . .

Ah . . . sweet sorrow . . .
what is there to be gained
by teasing me to tears with evasive joy
amongst my heart-strings?

My constant longing
for only you . . . dear God . . .
stands in my way, restricts my progress.

Erase this agitation of desire, Oh God.
Help me help myself
to cast aside this longing . . .
for desire is not the path, nor the truth,
and only You are the Way.

Long I wait for release to come,
as desire lingers in the wings. . . .
Then, quieting my longing down,
I faintly hear my soul sing . . .
releasing me to simply be.

Amidst the sweet and sour of my dream,
where God displaces time and thought,
an all-pervading Oneness
simply comes. . . .

Suddenly I felt cold, as if a wave of frigid wind blew through me. Yogananda was before me; his lips were not moving, but his message was clear. . . .

"Set aside the longing in these moments of rapture, and the pain of it will vanish. Swim in the moment.

"Longing is a desire for something you do not have. By saying you 'only desire God', you are acknowledging, in some degree, separation from God. Even to have a goal of 'going to God' or 'wanting to achieve God-realization' implies God is separate from your self.

"Words are a form of manifestation. Be careful not to manifest separation through the longing, for it conflicts with oneness. Quench the burning longing to a warm glow and attend to God. Think not of desire."

Then after a hesitation, he added:

"Accept the rapture; it is a gift."

His words reverberated in my heart, while at the same time, I became aware of myself as omnipresent, immortal spirit—wiser by far than my mortal self—who already knew that God and I are one, no separation. I have been, I am still, and I always will be in the eternal present, wholly absorbed in Him—in a world that lies within and without, in the absence of space and yet spacious, a world without tangible form but far more real.

A shiver of warmth flowed upward from the base of my spine and filled me. No longer did I feel possessed by the longing. As I write this, in my heart I sing over and over, *"A thousand Vedas do declare, 'Divine Mother is everywhere.'"*[36]

---

36   From the chant "Will That Day Come to Me, Mother?", *Cosmic Chants*, Paramahansa Yogananda, Self-Realization Fellowship.

Chapter Twelve

AWAKE IN GOD

I relive memories to write of,
giving form to my earthly purpose,
which holds me caged in flesh
to contemplate life away.

There is meaning
in these mystic pieces of life . . .
solutions for our suffering,
with hope for tomorrow.

After my heart attack, I had to take part in cardiac rehabilitation, just as I had done after the kundalini energy
awakening in 1998, which left me physically impaired.

Cardiac rehabilitation involved a room full of patients exercising on either a bike or a treadmill, all of them positioned
toward a television. News of the war in Iraq was the favored
item to watch. I soon felt so overwhelmed by the war news
that I scrambled to get off the exercise bike, nearly falling,
and cried out, "I can't do this. What kind of cardiac rehabilitation is this, when we have to watch such tragedy while
exercising? I simply cannot do it!"

I was shaking when I left and very disturbed by all that happened, including my own outburst. I knew I had to have the
therapy, but I knew that showing distressing news on television
was not a good environment for people in cardiac rehabilitation.

They called me on the phone when I got home and promised that the next time I came in they would have something else on the television, and from then on it was sitcoms. I could deal with that.

I am more sensitive to disturbing events now, having visited heaven. I try to avoid them, for the energy of such happenings penetrates our hearts and lowers our vibrations, and we in turn lower the vibrations of others.

When I see all the suffering in the world and grieve in rhythm with all who suffer, it detracts from my own peace. No matter how well I can interpret and understand the reasons for the suffering, I cannot remain a cool observer with a heart of ice, lost in my metaphysical heights and deaf to the cries of anguish ringing from so many corners of the earth.

Every gun that is made, every warship launched, every rocket fired signifies, in the final sense, a theft from those who hunger and are not fed, those who are cold and are not clothed.[37]

We can minimize the negative impact of watching violence on television by limiting our exposure to it and by concentrating instead on that which is good; for example, meditating on God, taking a walk to enjoy the fresh air, trees, flowers and sunshine, or reading a book that teaches wisdom or inspires unconditional love. Such activities raise our vibrations and consequently attract more good into our lives.

Still, we are not in this physical reality to ignore its disturbing aspects. Television news can help us to know what is happening around the world and in our own country so we

---

37   Spoken by President Dwight D. Eisenhower

can determine where to direct prayers, help where we can, and make informed decisions.

I wish there was a knob on the television to turn up the intelligence. There is one called "brightness", but it doesn't work.

———◇◇◇———

Not long after my near-death experience, I read that some scientists believe these experiences are caused by neuronal activity during trauma to the brain. If my experience had proceeded from neuronal activity, it would have mirrored the kinds of experiences and thoughts I have had throughout my life, which are stored in the brain and remembered later on, but this experience—giving rise to such extreme longing—far surpassed anything I had ever felt on this earth plane.

There are many reports of near-death experiences, and each person's is unique, for each of us has different desires and is at a different place on our path to God. It is my opinion that those who hover nearby are still strongly attached to the earth plane. Those who see other loved ones in a near-death experience do so because that is what they want to see when they die. I have always wanted to simply be with God.

An SRF monk said he believed it was my soul that experienced what I felt and saw when I left my body and went to heaven during my heart attack. My own belief concurred with his. Through my soul's memory, I can tell you what I remember of the experience.

Years back, while I was writing *Messages from Jesus*, I asked Jesus, "When liberated, is all sense of self gone? Is there still self?"

He answered, *"How would you know you were in paradise if there was no awareness? However, this awareness is without dualism, or distinctive separations. All is truly unified as one— as the great I AM—and within this paradise you dwell as pure, egoless soul, forever, with God."*[38]

In paradise, as soul, I am beyond the duality of ego-consciousness. I am awake in God—in the timelessness of eternity. As soul, I exist always and never do I not exist.

Jesus, ever present, is saying, *"God can summon you out of eternity at any time to reincarnate, for your soul essence is never lost. God knows each spark of being from the beginning of time. Thus anyone, including saints and healers of the universe, can be re-manifested whenever The Infinite so decrees."*

I rested in His words. For some reason this was very comforting to me.

<hr>

Recently, I received a phone call from a gentleman who said, "I understand you are the person I am supposed to call!" He went on to say his mother was very recently diagnosed with cancer and they were taking her to Grand Rapids for aggressive treatments, and would I come to see her for a healing session before they left.

I arrived to find she was seriously ill and had been for

38   *Messages from Jesus,* Third edition, p. 271.

some time for reasons other than cancer. I realized immediately that this woman would not be alive for very long. I did some energy work on her to help her relax, and talked to her and her son for quite a while.

A few weeks went by and again he called me. He wanted me to come to the funeral home where his mother was. He said, "I want to thank you. You were such a big help to my mother."

On my way to the funeral home, I tried to go over in my mind what I might have said to her in that short visit that was of such help. I couldn't remember what I said.

Upon arrival at the funeral home, the son told me that I had talked to her about dying and told her of my thoughts and experiences of heaven. Also, I did not sugar coat the process of dying, but emphasized heaven to come. Thus she was unafraid of the process. He also said, "No one else talked to her of dying! No one else had prepared her!"

It amazes me that at the end of life, when work is done and a rest is earned, there is little help with addressing the dying process and afterlife for those who need it.

This is one reason I am writing this book. I want people to know that there is life after death and there is nothing to fear.

Chapter Thirteen

CAREGIVING

Search me, O God, and know my heart;
test me and know my anxious thoughts.
See if there is any offensive way in me,
and lead me in the way everlasting.
—Psalm 139:23-24

My mother often talked of wanting to see Dad and her mother and father and other loved ones in the hereafter. That was her concept of heaven.

She was getting older and having more and more difficulty being on her own. It was hard for her to do her usual daily chores, and she had heart and hip challenges. One day, she announced that she planned on moving out of her apartment into a foster care home of her choosing. She adamantly refused to come and live with us. In her conservative mind, she considered Song of the Morning a cult! Nothing I could say would convince her otherwise.

She lived in foster care for several years until the foster home was sold. Mom was not happy with the care provided by the new owners and was not doing well physically. She needed more care than they were willing to provide, so she asked if she could come and live with us. I pondered her negative feelings about the Retreat, but in the end, I could not refuse her, for by taking me in as a small child, she had given me opportunities I otherwise might not have had.

Full-time caregiving immediately limited my husband's and my external freedoms. Many things had to be taken into consideration. She could not be left alone, her mobility was limited, she was on a restricted diet, and medication had to be given appropriately.

Even so, I felt it an honor to have this opportunity to care for her. It was the best of times and the worst of times. Her new doctor in our area immediately ordered hospice for her. We had aides, nurses, a social worker, a spiritual counselor, and a pastor coming to the house. It became a busy place. A volunteer came once a week, so we could get groceries and go out to lunch.

She often had visits from deceased friends and family members. "Don't you see them?" she would say, as she pointed to empty spaces. "You see Jesus; why can't you see them?" Truly the visits were meant for her, not for me, for her concept of heaven was that she would see her long-gone family and friends, and they would be there to greet her.

One day, after she had been with us nine months, I wheeled her in her wheelchair to the dining-room table, where she ate her meals. I set her lunch before her and turned back to the stove to get my own. Suddenly, she started screaming loud, unwarranted accusations and obscenities at me.

This was new. She was confused by her own hollering and couldn't seem to stop. Frustrated, she wanted to talk to George, but wasn't able to control her outbursts and words failed her. While she continued to scream at me, we got her into bed, wary of being hit by her. I called hospice, and they sent out a nurse.

It appeared that she had had a small stroke that affected her mind. She continued her ranting every time I came within view. I was devastated. All I could think of was that she must surely have been thinking these negative thoughts right along and maybe they were lodged in her subconscious mind. I had a hard time dealing with it.

My battle was trying to see her as the loving person she could be—as she rained obscenities on me—knowing all the while that one is capable of destroying even the closest relationship with a single harsh statement. I sometimes felt she was reaching out trying to say loving words, but the opposite just came spilling out. I continued to assure her of my love for her.

We made her as comfortable as we could. I played my CD of hymns, which I had recorded some time ago and which she had always loved, over and over for her. I stayed at her side through the days and nights, trying to soothe her, for she was progressively nearing death. Gasping for air for days, she clung to life and would not let go.

One night, before settling myself in the chair next to her bed, I went up to her and said, "Thank you for giving me a better chance at life by adopting me." She stopped her gasping to listen. . . . I continued, "I hope you will forgive me for all that I might have said or done that caused you grief. Also, Mom, I forgive you for all that you have said or done that upset me or George."

My mother had never apologized for anything she had ever done. She always said, "Love means you never have to say you're sorry."

Having listened to me, she took one long breath, and I knew she was leaving her body; and with a few more quiet breaths, she passed over. I stood there for a long time, trying to accept that one moment she was here and the next gone.

I truly believe she had been waiting for those words of forgiveness before leaving. Still, even with giving my mother what she needed to hear, I still held the memory of the obscenities she rained on me. And since I was still attached to her, it lay heavy on me.

I knew, from the experience with my first husband, that when we put off heartfelt forgiveness of others and even ourselves, the burden of our bitterness weighs upon us. It places us in the same category as the wrongdoer and darkens our lives until it is lightened with forgiveness, which truly has the power to heal.

I could only pray that she did not sense the incompleteness of my forgiveness and that she found her heaven, for I truly loved her.

While writing these words about my mother, Yogananda suddenly came into my mind, as if I had called on him. He set a message into my heart, gently, filled with love, as if it were poured from his heart.

"Little Mother, ten thousand, thousand mantras have I sung for you."

Tears came and bliss permeated my being and stilled my breath. Only after a few moments could I address his words.

"Ah, Sri Yogananda, as I write your sweet words my very being is close to God."

Yogananda continued, *"That is as it should be."*

There was a pause, a nothingness that seemed to sit on a fence for ever so long.

Then Yogananda conveyed, *"There are references to more than one heaven in the Bible. Your kind mother was awarded a heaven, fitting for her, that she so desired."*

With his words, I felt a wave of peace knowing that my mother went to the heaven she wanted—to join her long-gone family and friends, waiting at heaven's door to greet her.

When Jesus explained heaven to me in *Messages from Jesus*[39], it was the first time I had heard about more than one heaven. And, from what Yogananda said, I felt that he expected me to find the Bible passages referring to different heavens. I took my time to look them up and found several.

The Lord said to Moses, *"Behold, to the Lord your God belong heaven and the heaven of heavens, the earth with all that is in it."*[40]

Behold, heaven and the highest heaven cannot contain Thee. . . .[41]

But who is able to build Him a house, since heaven, even highest heaven, cannot contain Him?[42]

Behold, heaven and the highest heaven cannot contain Thee; how much less this house which I have built![43]

Jesus said to His disciples, *"In my Father's house are many*

39   *Messages from Jesus,* pp. 267-276
40   Deuteronomy 10:14
41   1 Kings 8:27
42   2 Chronicles 2:6
43   2 Chronicles 6:18

mansions; if it were not so, would I have told you that I go to prepare a place for you?"[44]

I believe these mansions are heavenly dwelling places—heavenly planes of consciousness—each mansion befitting the state of consciousness of the souls that go there.

Jesus said in *Messages from Jesus,* *"Once you can release yourself of every desire, experience the oneness above and beyond the perceived dualism of all the realms, and surrender the self, only then will your soul be one with God, for unless a soul be perfected, one cannot enter the highest heaven with God."*[45]

Yogananda came again, or maybe he never left, *"Anyone who is a God-realized person, limited in the end days by the mortal body or mind, God-realization will not be taken away from them, and they too will go to the Lord in the hereafter.*

"A person may be awarded a high heaven even if, at the very last moment, they genuinely realize the love of God after a lifetime of wrong thinking and actions.

"The criminal, while hanging from a cross next to Jesus during the crucifixion, repented and asked Jesus to remember him when He came into His kingdom. Jesus responded, 'Truly, I say to you, today you will be with me in Paradise.'[46]

"It is important to use this lifetime to lessen karma so the burden in the next incarnation is minimized, or better yet, use this lifetime to prevent the necessity of working out, in a reincarnation, any remaining karma."

I started thinking of the parable of the vineyard, wherein

44   John 14:2
45   *Messages from Jesus,* Third edition, p. 259.
46   Luke 43: 40-43.

Jesus said, *"For the kingdom of heaven is like a householder. . . ."* The householder offered to pay a denarius a day for laborers. Throughout the day he hired people, but at the end of the day they all received equal pay. Some grumbled, *"These last worked only one hour and you have made them equal to us who have borne the burden of the day, and the scorching heat."*[47]

I understand the parable better now, and it supports what Yogananda said, that a person may be awarded a high heaven even if, at the very last moment, they genuinely realize the love of God after a lifetime of wrong thinking and actions.

My mother had planned her own funeral—a quick, simple one with only family attending. At the funeral home, when all was said and done, a cousin said to me, "I have a book of family records your mother gave me. I am sure you have one too. One of us has to keep the records of births, marriages and deaths current."

I looked deep within her—remembering the times I was reminded that I was adopted and not real family—and with words that seemed to come from somewhere else, I said, "I don't know what you are talking about; I don't have any such thing. Apparently Mom gave it to you because she considered you more family than I, since I was adopted. So I think you should do it."

With those words, I immediately heard the sound of music from one of Yogananda's chants, filling me with sweetness. It was as if angels were singing:

"Father, mother, have I none.

---

47   Matthew 20: 1-16

I am He, I am He, Blessed Spirit, I am He!"

A rose fragrance entered my being like a waft of incense, removing what sorrow was left and filling me with joy. The words resonated within me, and with a freeing feeling of renunciation, I realized I was letting my mother go; truly forgiving her and myself. She was free from her attachment to me, and I was no longer attached to her. There was only love and fond memories.

Chapter Fourteen

SELF-REALIZATION

In my heart lies my meditation sanctuary.
Often, I find myself at its door
and pause for respite from a busy day,
worrisome but with reverent mind,
while earthly sounds seem far away.

I drop the worry outside the door
and step within, as on a hallowed path
leading to a place revered.
Each step I take I place with care;
I go to where my slate is cleared.

Years ago, when I was a practicing, conservative Christian, we talked about being saved, as if it were a given that we were going to heaven. We didn't talk of Self-realization, a word I had never heard.

Yogananda speaks of "Self-realization" in his writings. By "Self-realization", he means salvation, or liberation from the delusion of dualistic consciousness.

In contrast, for those who did not go to heaven, it seemed as though hell, as eternal punishment, might be in store for them. But I have grown away from that thinking. I believe that eternal punishment is non-existent, for we learn lessons from wrong as well as good actions in each lifetime—in the physical, astral and causal worlds—growing in love and wisdom as we draw ever closer to God.

Eternal punishment would have no place in God's plan, for God wishes to redeem every soul He has created. Besides, a loving father would never punish his children eternally, and it makes no sense to think that God, whose love is infinite, would do this.

After many lifetimes, one becomes aware that there is more out there, hidden in plain sight. You find that sacredness exists in the midst of life. You begin to honor Mother Nature and all she holds in her keep. You strive to do what is right and true and loving. You begin to let go of what no longer serves you and begin a conscious search for The Divine. You learn to meditate and commune with God.

As you progress, you follow inner guidance more and more, accepting doctrines that seem to be true in the light of your inner knowing and rejecting those you feel no longer serve you.

You abhor negativity. You desire the highest good for all. You see goodness and purpose in all creation, all people; and you feel everywhere the presence of God. You are in the world but not of it.

> The world goes on. Souls come and go.
> Delusion haunts them for a time. . . .
> Then, leaving little joys for greater,
> some choose to soar in lofty flight,
> like mighty eagles, in the light.
>
> —George Johnston

As you awaken into a higher life, you may receive gifts of increased creativity, joy, divine fragrances, visions, healing and more. I received my healing gift during this phase of my life. It was a time of joyful surrender and great contentment.

Even as we grow in awareness of God, our efforts to progress are challenged by earthly desires and habits, which keep us engrossed in the physical aspects of the world and often limit our awareness of its spiritual dimensions. If our desires are expressed in unloving or selfish ways, they hurt us and cause harm to others, thus creating negative karma that has to be worked out through difficult experiences later on, usually in another lifetime.

Our challenging and painful experiences in life are often for the purpose of balancing past karma, although we may not recognize them as such. But by dealing with every situation in a wise and loving way, this karma is balanced and negative karma is not created.

Living a loving, caring life in service to God, family and humanity helps us to expand the boundaries of our compassion and feel that we are one with all. By living in love, we become happier and more peaceful within.

Fortunately, the peace, love and bliss that we experience as we grow spiritually are far more enjoyable than the physical pleasures of the senses, and once we have tasted the joys of the soul, we want to experience more of the same and to overcome any worldly tendencies that stand in the way.

Thus, as you can see, our lives are an ongoing battle between the divine impulse to grow spiritually and realize our oneness with God, and the habits and desires of our lower self, or ego.

In the quest for Self- (or God-) realization, many seekers take up the practice of meditation in order to experience the love, light and bliss of God in the silence of the soul. One might even experience a spiritual awakening, as I did on the morning of the 1998 New Year, when I was catapulted into ever higher dimensions of awareness as intense energy rose up my spine.[48] I became more aware of the life, intelligence and beauty in nature, I more often smelled fragrances with nothing in my surroundings to explain them, and my world was often haloed in supernal light—what I call 'brilliance seeing'. I felt closer to God than I ever had before and began to write poetry about the spiritual experiences and visions that were coming to me. To this day, the blessings of that awakening are still with me.

One's inmost Self—the perfect essence of the soul—can be likened unto a beautiful, unblemished crystal hidden in the earth, awaiting discovery. On finding the crystal and then contemplating it deeply, one is able eventually to receive the benefit of the beauty, knowledge and power within it. So also, by searching for the Self in the cave of meditation, we discover it, and by contemplating it deeply, eventually receive its knowledge and power, and experience in it the peace, love, light and joy of God. In time, we realize that our Self is immortal and omnipresent, one with all things, all beings, and God.

Addressing Yogananda as if he were with me ...

"I believe Self-realization is knowing that we live in the presence of and are at one with God and creation, and do not

48   *Sustained by Faith*, pp. 107-118. *Messages from Jesus*, Third edition, pp. 20-21.

have to ask for this oneness to come to us, for it is with us always, awaiting remembrance."

"That is true," Yogananda reverberated in my heart.

"I believe that we can simply know we are one with God and be Self-realized, once we can diminish the illusion of separateness from God.

"I am a child of God; I know that God and I have always been one. It is a knowing in my heart, not from intellectual knowledge but from heart-felt, personal experience. Still, I am not fully liberated because my ego challenges me.[49] Thus, I feel as though I am on the brink between duality and full liberation—like the sun as it hesitates, before rising up over the horizon at dawn."

"The ego thrives on attention. Let go and let God shine forth.

"You are God expressed—an essence of God, worthy of all there is—every one of you. Know this ... believe it ... remember it."

"I remember when, a few years back, you told me to go with the knowing, and recently you reminded me of this again, *'Go with the knowing.'*[50]

"This wisdom is known in the Self—and can be remembered by a process of divine recollection."

His words rolled over me, as a cool breeze coming from out of the west. Sweetness came over me while I went on.

---

49   The ego aspect of the mind keeps us from fully experiencing the love and oneness of God, because it thinks only in terms of separation, opposites and contrasts. It causes us to identify with our body instead of the omnipresent Self and to see ourselves as separate from each other and God. Through meditation, loving thoughts, and spiritual living, the dualistic, materialistic thoughts of the ego are replaced with ever-greater realizations of unity, wholeness, and harmony.

50   *Sustained by Faith,* p. 187

"It amazes me to hear people say, 'I wish I were realized!' I don't think people realize they already are realized."[51]

I could sense Yogananda's deep, exuberant laughter, and out came, *"I realize that!"*

Laughing with him, I went on . . .

"I had another brush with death very recently. My heart slowed down to an unstable pace and quit for just a moment in time, but there was no heavenly visit. Modern science stepped in and saved my life. I have a pacemaker; I named her Grace.

"At one point during the ordeal, you and Jesus and my mother were standing by me. It was a comforting feeling."

"It wasn't your time to go. You and George are in the midst of a great work. I say great, because of the spirit of truth lying within you. All truth has greatness. The world needs all writings of truth at this time of tribulation—yours, and from others who are writing, and those already written—to remind people that God is your very being, a loving God, and to go forth as such."

I thought of what he said, for a while, and then I felt that his words held no burden for me. They were light and weightless, full of love. I felt free. I went into my heart's meditation room and was there for a long time.

> *I find within a quiet place,*
> *where I can be one with all*
> *in God's sustaining grace.*

---

51 Yogananda understood my meaning more deeply than what is expressed in these words. What I meant is that people already are realized, in the sense that the Self already is one with God.

The pacemaker does not allow me to slow my heart rate down, for it is preset at a specific range to sustain my heart. Thus, in order to go deep during meditation, I separate myself from my physical body.

"I once went to a conference where we took turns standing up in front of everyone to state an intention. I had no idea what I was going to say, but when it was my turn, I hesitatingly went to the front of the room where, not in control of myself, my arms were thrown open and I found myself loudly proclaiming, 'I give myself permission to be Self-realized!'

"I stood immobile for a while, not oriented to the room, not aware that my arms were still outstretched. I was rooted in place. I heard people gasp as if I had sworn. When the presenter started talking, his voice seemed to be coming from every direction. It took me a moment to find him in the room. Only then could I bring my arms to my side."

"The lila of Divine Rapture made itself known for you."

"Oh, the realization of something so huge as God can be but light and playful and yet so deep."

As I write this, Yogananda is whispering into my heart, *"Truth set you free, and you were opened to the universe, and you let go, and what came forth is exactly what those people needed to hear. This is what I have been saying to you, 'let go and let God.'"*

I took a deep breath, held it, and then it seemed to be drawn upward by some invisible force, leaving me boundless.

Then, as if in a time warp, the following words from Yogananda reverberated in my mortal being, mixing with and bringing me out of the ecstasy.

"Breath reveals unity in God."

It took me a moment to give his words some thought for I felt ungrounded.

"My breath often triggers a rise into a higher state of consciousness—oneness. I don't know how else to explain it.

"Often I quiet my mind during the day, in short periods of silence, to breathe through my mind and astral and physical bodies. This breath play opens me to meditation."

"What you are doing is a form of kriya you learned in past lifetimes. It is innate within you. It is enough."

Feeling relieved that Yogananda accepted my breath play as "enough" for me, I took a deep cleansing breath and sighed it out.

"Still, I realize we are here for this great experience and must be able to make adjustments to achieve balance between duality and oneness in our lives and be physically and mentally present for it."

"True, but while living in this world, don't become attached to that which is perishable. For now, enjoy it, learn from it, but above all, see God in it."

Then suddenly, in my mind's eye, Babaji was before me, as if he parted a curtain and stepped forth. Instantly I knew who he was. I unexpectedly felt as if maybe he had taught me my breath play in this lifetime, though up to then I had thought Jesus did, and maybe Yogananda.

"One and the same," I heard above my thoughts. *"And many lifetimes ago."*

Like a star within myself, the words "Babaji Maharaj" echoed in my mind, over and over, like a mantra dancing in light. I saw myself pranamed before him, lost for a time.

Then Babaji placed an open book before me—it had a brilliant aura all its own. Crisp, black writing on pure, white, shining paper jumped out at me, and out of the recesses of my mind, I recognized the writing as directives he had given me several years ago. I only used them for a class pertaining to manifestation. Now, I realized this was encouragement to share them in this book.

> ~ All that you need is already yours
>   to create in your life. ~
> ~ Trust in your own divine self,
>   and your needs will be few. ~
> ~ Ask little for yourself,
>   and you will receive abundance. ~
> ~ Know God as One with yourself,
>   and creation will manifest for you. ~
> ~ Light up the world with your gratefulness. ~
> ~ You are the perfect manifestation
>   of God consciousness. ~
> ~ Only be happy. ~

Yogananda, Babaji, and the vision faded from me, while I thought how simple Babaji's directives really are, if only simple were not so hard.

I didn't have time to even think about Babaji's departure, for my pelvic floor suddenly clamped shut, forming a chalice for the shiver of energy that seemingly boiled within—in a God-filled swirl—upwards from the base of my spine, flowing into every crevice of my body and out the top of my head.

Chapter Fifteen

ONLY BE HAPPY

If you want others to be happy,
practice compassion.
If you want to be happy,
practice compassion.

—Dalai Lama

O f all the directives that Babaji gave us, "Only be Happy" is the one I ponder most often. People spend a lifetime searching for lasting happiness and rarely find it. They don't realize the search is within.

"Who looks outside, dreams.
Who looks inside, awakens."[52]

Most people try to find happiness in physical pleasures—entertainment, eating and sex, for example —and by accumulating possessions, sometimes at the cost of the well-being of others. One may succeed in getting what one wants, but as soon as one desire is satisfied, another always comes to the fore, and one is caught up in seemingly endless cycles: cravings, followed by either satisfaction or frustration, followed by renewed or different cravings. The lure of material happiness causes one to become engrossed in these cycles, which are accompanied by pleasure, pain, fear, and sometimes anger, depending on how things pan out. Such is the

---

52   Carl Gustav Jung, Swiss psychiatrist, psychologist and founder of
Analytical Psychology, 1875-1961.

dualistic nature of this world, where pain and pleasure follow one another and sometimes are intermixed.

Moreover, if we live too much on the sense plane, always seeking physical pleasures and acquiring things, our minds are too restless for us to calmly focus on, and thus be able to fully enjoy, the physical pleasures and things we already have. And, even if we were able to fully enjoy them, physical pleasures and things cannot fulfill our inner longing for peace, joy and bliss.

Fortunately, there comes a time when, through tragedy, pain or disillusionment, we call on God, step out of our rut, and start searching for a better way to live. We may catch a glimpse of goodness from some kind heart or have a spiritual epiphany that sets us on a path toward God. Then happiness starts to slip in—like fresh air through an open window.

To be happy, we need to feel loved. God sees every one of us, not as we see ourselves, but as His children created out of His own divine substance, and loves us all. God does not play favorites. His love has no boundaries and encompasses everyone.

If you want happiness, make others happy. Happiness comes back to you when your work and words are for the benefit of others. We make a living by what we get, but we make a life by what we give. Happiness is in each present moment when we leave self-centered thoughts behind and create happiness for others.

I once worked in a nursing home and was in a situation where two nurse aides were witness to my instant calming of a resident through energy work with her. They reported me, and it raised skepticism within the nursing staff. I went home upset and angry, and during the night God reminded me, *"Whatever you do, do it with love."*

The next day was beautifully played out. I saw the nurse aides and sincerely felt nothing but love for them. Before I could say anything to them they were apologizing to me. We ended up laughing at our initial responses to the situation, and there was born a sweet bond between myself and the nurse aides, and it grew to include other staff.

I explained the benefits of energy work to the nursing staff at a meeting, and was given permission to use it with residents when moved to do so. This is what love does.

In your inmost essence—the Self—you are love, and with love all things are possible. Love heals discord within ourselves and in our relationships with others, counteracts fear and other happiness-destroying emotions, and bestows peace of mind, contentment and joy. It is the best incentive and guide for moral behavior and brings us ever closer to God. The happiness love brings is far beyond what the world has to offer.

Even so, happiness is hard to hold onto when dark clouds of negative thinking threaten to take away our peace of mind, or when temptation knocks at the door. It is important to cultivate self-control and strength of character, so we can stay positive when things "go wrong", and resist temptation and bad habits, which cause suffering for oneself and others later on.

Happiness needs to be constantly nourished through un-conditional love of self and others, forgiveness, constructive thoughts, gratitude and appreciation. Choose and practice the things that create happiness and avoid those that promise happiness but ultimately destroy it.

Happiness also depends on the physical necessities required for our role in life. To provide for these needs, most of us have to work and keep abreast of changes in the world around us. When our basic, material needs and those of our dependents are met, and when we practice self-control and do what we know is right, rather than giving in to blind desires, we have a strong foundation for happiness.

Even if your needs are not being met, you can still be happy if you feel God's presence, no matter what the circumstance. When faith expands within you and radiates outward, you have the gift for making yourself and others happy, and your life will change.

As I have mentioned, we need to purify our minds of negative thoughts and inclinations, draw closer to God, and live in harmony with God's laws of moral behavior in order to have lasting happiness. Reading truths expressed in scriptures and sacred writings, contemplating them, and sharing them with those who are receptive, give us wisdom and motivation to do this.

In the same vein, seeking inwardly for God's guidance by learning to discern the promptings of Spirit within us—as true intuition, or the "inner voice"—and acting on this guidance also leads to happiness.

Thus sacred teachings and divine inner guidance may be considered as directives that lead to happiness. For God wants only the best for all of us.

When we choose to live our life as an expression of gratitude and love, and follow the intuitive guidance of Spirit within us, we begin to experience more fully the joy of a higher life, a life filled with the presence of God. And as we grow in moral strength, emotional stability, and spiritual awareness, we become much happier and are able to stay cheerful when difficulties come into our life and threaten to take our happiness away.

Although God-knowing saints, masters, avatars, and good Samaritans[53] often endure great difficulties in order to serve humanity, they experience the peace, love and joy of God, and have an inner happiness that sustains them. They live to do God's work, and God supplies their needs. Buoyed up and energized by Spirit, they uplift those around them and many have a keen sense of humor. They don't often have long faces. As Saint Francis de Sales said, "A saint who is sad is a sad saint."

God is bliss, and when we feel God in our hearts, we find joy in everyday life and are able to laugh at the amusing incongruities in life. Sometimes mirth bubbles up within us and we smile, without even knowing why.

The conditions I have mentioned that contribute to happiness are much more easily fulfilled if we meditate. For meditation connects us with the Divine Source of the love, inner strength, and wisdom that we need in order to fulfill these conditions. In addition, meditation creates happiness in and of itself, because when we meditate, we leave all troubles behind, dwell in stillness and peace, and commune in love—sometimes even bliss—with our eternal Father-Mother-God.

53   Luke 10:30-37.

In meditation, we strive to withdraw our consciousness, or awareness, from physical sensations and the mental activity of thinking, which keep most of us from experiencing spiritual reality. Like veils, they usually block one's awareness of higher worlds, the Self and God.

Mentally repeating a sacred sound, phrase or prayer is a way to withdraw one's consciousness from thoughts of the world and direct it toward God. I often mentally repeat, over and over, a mantra, such as "Oh, God Beautiful", or the Gayatri mantra, or simply "God, God, God."

While mentally repeating a mantra with closed eyes, one may also focus one's attention on the "third eye" (the sixth chakra at the point between the eyebrows) or the heart chakra.

If you learn to control breath and life force through a technique of pranayama, you may be able to stop the distracting flow sensations and constantly changing thoughts and emotions, and enter the realm of absolute stillness, the altar of God.

On taking up the practice of meditation and observing the changing thoughts and feelings that arise in the mind, one may be put off on discovering just how restless their mind is. However, mental restlessness is the norm unless one has been meditating regularly for some time. Eventually, one is able to quiet their mind to a greater or lesser extent, and even if it was still somewhat active during meditation, they feel relaxed, calm and refreshed afterward. Of course, you should always try to still your mind completely, go deep and know God as one with yourself.

Be still and know
that I am God.[54]

Techniques performed with clear intent can enable you to leave behind all sensory distractions, worries, fears and cares, go beyond thinking, and deeply concentrate on some aspect of God. Then, in the silent sanctuary of pure awareness, it is possible through love and devotion to have communion with and direct experience of The Divine.

However, if you have been practicing certain meditation techniques and they don't appear to be helping you, perhaps because of health challenges or for some other reason, you should consider finding new techniques or relying more on other ways of connecting with God.

Jesus said to me some time ago, *"It matters not by what manner you arrive in God consciousness."*

In deciding what to do, seek guidance, either as intuitive promptings from Spirit or from someone whose wisdom you trust, because it is all too easy to give up one's practices prematurely, when by persevering, you might overcome obstacles that stand in your way.

When I have physical difficulties, I simply sit in meditative silence, praying or talking to God . . .

no techniques,
no right way or wrong way,
just being alone in God.

Be patient with yourself. Even as those who meditate sometimes despair of achieving the illumination they seek,

54   Psalm 46:10.

just by making the effort to quiet the roaming mind, they are making progress and changing within, becoming more intuitive and perceptive, more peaceful and assured, more aware of God's guidance and help in their daily lives.

Moreover, those, myself included, who have experiences of being fully alive in God often go through periods when there are no blissful experiences or deep meditations. Just as there are cycles and rhythms in nature, so too, our spiritual life has its ups and downs and lulls. Then suddenly, one day, there comes a deep meditation, a visitation, new insight, or a loving realization of God.

I have learned, over the years, to let go of expectations for deep meditations or spiritual experiences when they seem to be on hold. I simply take a little sabbatical from worrying about this and am grateful for what I have received. I have a high respect for those who do not have spiritual visions or experiences, yet steadfastly meditate daily. The peace they find in meditation benefits everyone, for its high vibration changes them within and radiates out into the world.

For several years, in addition to silent meditation, I have practiced what I call wakeful meditation, wherein I experience all things in one vaporous flow of love and light, all while my mortal self, weighted down by ego, engages in physical and mental activities in dualistic consciousness.

Wakeful meditation is a form of meditative awareness during daily activities, in which one does not have to be in stillness and silence in order to be in God consciousness.

Brother Lawrence said, *"The time of work does not with me differ from the time of prayer. In the noise and clatter of my kitchen, while several persons are at the same time calling for different things, I possess God in as great a tranquility as if I were upon my knees at the Blessed Supper."*[55]

———— ❧ ————

I tell you of my experiences to show what can come to us in our search for God. Many of you have had your own spiritual experiences that brought you closer to God and deepened your faith. They may have been very different from mine, for each of us has different needs and a unique personal relationship with God.

If you live in love, seeking God in earnest without giving up no matter how difficult your challenges may be, you overcome past bad karma and get glimpses of divinity. Then, as you progress, guided by Spirit, you begin to abide in and merge with the peace, love, light, and bliss of God. This is the highest, the most enduring and joyful kind of happiness there is.

---

55   *The Practice of the Presence of God: Brother Lawrence's Conversations and Letters,* Light Heart Edition. www.PracticeGod'sPresence.com.

Chapter Sixteen

MANIFESTATION

Know God as one with yourself,
and creation will manifest for you.
                                —Mahavatar Babaji

I woke up this morning and put a thought out into the universe that I wish today was Saturday instead of Sunday.

I took my shower and got myself dressed for Sunday service. When I was ready, I hollered at George, who was in the garage, that it was time to leave. He came running and asked if I was okay! Then he said, "It's Saturday!" Thank the universe! I manifested another wonderful thing; a whole extra day!

It is good that our lives offer us opportunity to laugh at ourselves. So, I simply changed my clothing, fixed breakfast, then went out to sit in the flower garden, where I am usually weeding, trimming and moving things about, but this time simply rest as if an invited guest.

> Ah ... the joy of garden keep—
> Moving this and adding that,
> Dirty hands and buzzing bees,
> Weeding things before they seed.

Trimming dead heads, bushes too,
Cleaning up all odds and ends,
Cutting herbs and drying them
For our kitchen and our friends.

Raccoons, hummingbirds and bees,
Petunia Skunk here to visit me,
Charlie Chipmunk, well at ease—
All get along beneath the trees.

This time of year has a feeling like the pause between breaths, an episode or hesitation between the glory of summer and the colorful display of autumn. Summer is truly over, but I had hardly noticed.

I too, am in the autumn of my life. It's as if my youth has gone away, and yet my life is not stagnant. My inner self is as alive and fresh with passion for God as ever it was.

I have time for those who want to talk or come for healing sessions. Time to comfort, time to listen, time for new learning and time for meditation and prayer—prayer expressing praise and love.

There is also time for my husband and me to enjoy each other, time to witness and be one with the unhurried pace of nature, time for family, time for reminiscing.

It suddenly seemed wondrous to me that my garden and I are sharing the world *this very present moment* with whales, airplanes, the homeless, mountains, tragedy, the pope, frogs, people in Egypt and Madrid, all creation. It was such a huge feeling—this wonder—I felt as though I were in a dream.

Generally I feel at one with my surroundings, but today it was as if all creation were in this present moment with my garden and me—God everywhere.

As I write this, I hear these words: *Oneness is most natural for those able to recognize God in everything and themselves.*

One evening a few years back, while my husband and I were sleeping, I woke up to the sound of a train in the distance. We don't have trains in the area. It grew louder and louder, and I suddenly remembered that the sound of a tornado can sound like a train. Realizing there was a great wind outside, I jumped up and threw my robe on.

I went to the living room, looked out the sliding glass doors and saw our giant trees bending drastically, and smaller trees seemed almost horizontal. Without thinking, I raised my arms and emphatically said to the wind, "Just calm down, just calm down". Then, as I slowly lowered my arms, the storm around me quieted. We didn't lose a single tree on our property; however, the 800-acre Retreat was strewn with fallen trees.

There was no doubt in my mind that the storm would quiet. There was no thought, no thinking about it. I simply responded instinctively to an inner, powerful urgency to calm the wind. It was like the sudden urgency that would sometimes come over me while working in a hospital or elsewhere, wherein I am moved by God to heal a certain person with His healing grace. If I don't follow through in some way, I suffer feelings of remorse.

If you look at and listen to what is right before you, without letting what you have been taught and conditioned to expect stand in the way of your innocent perception, you begin to see and hear and know much more than you previously were aware of. And communion in God in nature comes more easily.

We usually think in terms of physical cause and effect, expecting our needs to manifest as a result of physical causes. But we live in a state of grace that transcends physical causes, and need only to have faith that our thoughts, empowered by love and guided by intuition, can work miracles.

We choose to incorporate the "what if" and "but" and "can't" nonsense into our consciousness and worry too much about the "how" of things. This limits our ability to be open to manifesting legitimate needs through the power of Spirit. What we lovingly intend creates our experience. If we could learn to simply put a thought out into the universe with no attachment to outcome, and then, without wavering, let it go and allow the manifestation to occur in its own perfect way, achievement would be far easier. Move from the mind that only accepts what it is able to explain, to the mind that follows the wisdom of the heart.

Removing limiting thoughts from your mind takes practice, but it is the beginning of learning how to use your consciousness to create what you need.

Wake up your creative aliveness.
Dance with the wind—in your mind, body and heart.

Some will believe I manifested a quieted wind; others might think it was coincidence—a word that helps keep God's intervening power anonymous! Nevertheless, intentions do manifest into physical reality through Spirit in concert with you.

Jesus said, "*Manifestation comes with sound intentions.*"[56] A sound intention is clear of "hopefully" and "maybe" qualifiers, and other limiting thoughts. These manifest nothing. Ask in a positive way clear of attachment to outcome, for attachment interferes with manifestation.

A manifestation should be for the good of yourself and others and help one to grow stronger in love, self-reliance, wisdom or other good qualities. And, of course, in manifesting an intention, one should always be willing to work, using one's body, reason, will, and creativity.

An intention can take the form of asking the universe or God for help in fulfilling a genuine need. You might say:

> I need a job so that I can . . .
> > And you find a part-time or full time job.
> I need shelter for my family. . . .
> > And you find warmth in a homeless shelter or
> > some other place.
> I need relief from my challenges because . . .
> > And your challenges persist because you learn
> > from them.
> O God, please come into my life right now. . . .
> > And a person befriends you.

Your manifestations are the result of your words and actions as well as your intentional thoughts, and appear not only in your present lifetime, but as karmic effects that

56 *Messages from Jesus,* Third edition, p. 226.

blossom forth later on. I know poor people who share what little they have, and I know poor people who won't accept more than they can use. Such generosity will be returned to them in this or a future lifetime. Give out what you want to receive, including money, assistance, friendship, love, compassion and harmony.

If you don't believe in the manifesting power of intention, then you will be unable to consciously utilize it. But if you are open to believing in and recognizing the fulfillment of your sound intentions, they suddenly begin to work. I find that the more comfortable I am with the process, the more easily it flows.

Jesus said to me, *"If they doubt, there is no room for believing. . . . If they believe, there will be no room for doubt."*[57]

Many people confuse needs with wants. There is a mighty difference between the two, brought home to me by a mother and her child in a grocery store some time ago. The child was in a cart and was loudly, emphatically crying because she wanted something. The mother asked her if it was a want or a need. At this point, I could sense the small child's mind working as she stopped to think, then she realized the difference and quit her asking. Bless them both.

Babaji said, *"Trust in your own divine self, and your needs will be few."* When you trust in your divine self, you manifest simple, uncomplicated ways to live and be happy. Suppose you want to live a simple life, and although you wonder if you will be able to support yourself, you trust in your divine self to guide you day by day and help you fulfill your purpose in

57 *Messages from Jesus,* Third edition, p. 158.

life. From within your Self, Spirit guides you in finding work that provides for your physical needs, and you find happiness in quietude, simple pleasures, meditation, and spiritual study.

As you progress spiritually, you begin to let go of the non-essentials in life with the ease of wind through the trees. You take better care of yourself. You strive to live your life in harmony with the will of God by listening to and following your inner, intuitive knowing—the "voice of God" within you. You yearn not for God's earthly blessings, but for God. The more you taste God's love and bliss, the stronger your love for God becomes, and you receive the greatest gift of all—you *"know God as one with yourself."* Then, the yearning of your heart is satisfied, you are content, and whatever you need *"creation will manifest for you."*

"Consider the ravens: they neither sow nor reap, they have neither storehouse nor barn, and yet God feeds them. Of how much more value are you than the birds? And which of you by being anxious can add a cubit to his span of life? If then you are not able to do as small a thing as that, why are you anxious about the rest?

"Consider the lilies, how they grow; they neither toil nor spin; yet I tell you, even Solomon in all his glory was not arrayed like one of these. But if God so clothes the grass, which is alive in the field today, and tomorrow is thrown into the oven, how much more will he clothe you, O ye of little faith?

"And do not seek what you are to eat and what you are to drink, nor be of anxious mind. For all the nations of the world seek these things; and your Father knows that you need them. Instead, seek his kingdom, and these things shall be yours as well."[58]

---

58   Luke 12:22-31

Through gratitude we acknowledge God. Thank God for all things including creating you. Be grateful for what you are, for "*you are the perfect manifestation of God consciousness.*"

Gratitude is the great multiplier. When we are grateful for the blessings of life, the divine, magnetic power of the heart is strengthened, and this attracts even more good into our lives. With joy, thank God for all things, even the little things. And, "*light up the world with your gratefulness.*"

Chapter Seventeen

LIFE SONG

My life, given to me as a gift,
creates a melody,
and the mystical reality of it,
the singing.

I once heard a recording of pure, angelic, heavenly voices, which sounded like choirs toning in harmonies. The rise and fall of voices fading in and out gave the impression that there was no breath taken—no pause. They just seemed to go on and on in joyful song. The celestial voices and their vibrato resonated within me, penetrating my very spirit, and took me, soaring, into a meditative state.

This was a recording of the sound of crickets with their song slowed according to the ratio of their lifespan to that of a human! In nature few people would experience this. It only shows up with human technology.

"Ah, Saint Ta, There is music in the rhythm and cycles of all creation—like distinct voices and instruments in orchestra. Its collective vibration and light reflects back to God the state of the earth and those asleep in duality consciousness."

I was momentarily stunned. Out of the blue, Jesus speaks to me as if He were always listening, using an endearment I have not heard in quite a while.

Our life song is our state of consciousness—as we interact

with events in our life—created in our heart and mind and expressed through our words and actions. When we are in tune with God, it blesses others like a medley of colorful flowers in the field resurrected in the spring with ever-new life.

As we live in the broader concert of life—blending into and clashing here and there in response to each other's life songs—our lives play out in rhythm, with pianissimos into crescendos and back to pianissimos again, with pauses and speed, highs and lows, flats and sharps, minors and majors.

In the bright stanzas of our life we laugh, with melodies of joy in our voices. Other times we moan, with deep, flat resonances invading the beat of our hearts, intensifying our sorrow to build it up and purge it. Or we resoundingly scream from the very depths of our being, opening the floodgate of the heart, allowing us to express and release pent-up emotions.

The lulls between the spiritual highs in our lives are like musical episodes between each repetition of a major melodic theme. I often think of these lulls as episodes during which we grow in humility, faith, love, inner strength and wisdom through acts of forbearance, kindness, forgiveness and courage, and through gratitude, spiritual study, and perseverance in seeking to know and do God's will. These lulls may sometimes seem lacking in divine blessings, but spiritual qualities are being developed that, later on, fill our life songs with fresh arias of love.

Sing your life song with joy, pouring out from you in grateful praise for all the dips and highs given to you, for the length and breadth of all that you have learned, and as an expression of your compassion.

Music and fond memories of it have always been a companion to me—sweet hymns of my youth, songs I sang in musicals and choirs, playing piano for hours in the summer of my life, spiritual chants here in the autumn of my life, and impromptu melodies that arise in my heart while in communion with nature and God.

I have mentioned music in my writings but never gave it just praise. I do so now, for I am grateful for the gifts and grace of music in my life.

Music imitates the feelings and emotions that stir within us and are expressed outwardly in our life song. Because of its intimate connection with our body, mind and soul, music that resonates with us has healing power and helps us cope with life's challenges. It often brings peace to troubled minds, comforts a broken heart, helps those who are grieving, and distracts those in pain.

Spiritual music, when it touches the soul, can awaken divine love, transmit vibrations of bliss, and bring one into a state of communion with God.

Happy, lilting tunes lift us up, chase away gloom and sadness, and fill our hearts and minds with gaiety and cheer, mirth and exuberance.

Martial music gives us courage to stand up for what is right, gives us hope when all seems lost, and vanquishes our fears.

Music brings harmony where there is discord. It is a universal language that crosses national boundaries and helps bring people together. This universal language crosses nature's boundaries too. I sing in the garden or in the forest to express myself in nature or respond to its beckoning call. Sometimes when I sing with nature, inspirations emerge from out of a greater consciousness—upsurging from the ocean of Spirit—wherein personal roots and history mingle with universal collective singing.

Singing is healthy. By the time I'm through singing out loud, I feel good. I've breathed deeply and am more in touch with my Self and the present moment.

I once went to a metaphysical church in Lansing, Michigan. At one point they had us stand in a circle to sing Om. The instruction was that we could sing it on any note we felt comfortable with. It began in disharmony. As our impulses were freed and we melted into unity, out of the continued dissonance, the sounds became one sound, much like the Om sound as the earth spins through space—the sounds of all humanity with its harsh and sweet realities all wrapped up together into one.

It's wonderful to give praise and gratitude to God through singing. When I sing in nature, I feel the cadence of the constant beat of my heart and sometimes merge into oneness with the hum of the universal OM. Like wind through a pitch pipe, OM gives me the key—which never changes—in which to sing.

"Brave Heart, your singing gives pause to all listening ears. Wherever you are, I am.

"This is your last book. Write inspired thoughts when you want to. Sharing genuine inspiration is a gift to humanity. Offer

who you are. Those who act in the world as an example of divine love, thankfulness, and divine joy will be imitated by countless others."

Sweetness flowed through me, like an inner shower of bliss, and set me to rest in Jesus' words for a time. I expected this to be my last book, and yet I felt surprised to hear it from Jesus. With this book the story of my experiences with God and the masters is brought up to date, thus I see the reasoning to expect it to be the last one.

"Ah, Sweet Jesus, I am eternally thankful for your guidance and companionship in my life, and for all others who help me: Yogananda, Babaji, Sebastian, Archangel Arial, Sri Yukteswar, Jonathan, and my husband, George. I know it is not the end, for every day adds ever-new melodies to my life song and brings me closer to God.

"I feel as if I am swimming in the One, all while being fully present here on earth. I cannot express my gratitude in words. I can only express it through my heart. I love you, Sweet Jesus."

"Rest easy now . . .
Rest easy now."

The words were like an echoing round of music playing my soul. When I finally let go, I felt a soulful, joyful feeling, leaving me unable to respond. Ever-new joy . . .

Be still, my soul,

And let me meditate upon our God,

For no appointed time, but far beyond,

As God has come to turn my darkness into light

And deliver me into radiance to end my night.

Be still, my soul,

And know what God would have me see,

For I seek answers: Why and what made me to be?

But there is no sound and nothing to be heard;

I strain to hear, within the endless void, a word.

As false illusions, fear and longing fell away,

God's holy light changed darkness into day,

And somewhere . . . everywhere . . . above,

I heard God softly whisper . . . "Love."

The sound reverberated far in colorful light,

Which filled my eyeless sight.

While iridescent waves joined in playful flight,

My soul merged within the endless light.

Amidst the loving echoes of God's grace,

Worries of eternal boredom were erased,

And fantasies that seemed so real just yesterday

Were no longer in my way.

With love . . . my soul . . .

There is nothing more to know.

And for the world at rest within my heart,

I sing within, "My God, how wonderful Thou art."

INDEX

BOOKS BY MARY ANN JOHNSTON

SUSTAINED BY FAITH

"A powerful story of hope and courage! This book bears witness to the truth that even in the midst of darkness we can be filled with light. Mary Ann candidly and generously shares the details of a difficult life lived in the consciousness of the Holy Presence and in so doing uplifts and inspires us all."

—Marilyn Beker,
Senior Screenwriting Professor,
School of Film and Television,
Loyola Marymount University, Los Angeles, CA

MESSAGES FROM JESUS

"Chances are, if you have a question for Jesus, the answer lies in these pages, as the essence of the spiritual life, modern religion, world affairs, and disasters are all dealt with rather comprehensively.

"Nothing that I or the author could say will convince anyone skeptical of these pages' origin about their authenticity. But then again, only personal conviction will allow any scripture to be thought of as veritable. I encourage you to delve into this work and find out for yourself if Truth is present here. My guess is, regardless of what you determine, you won't skip a page."

—Fred Stella, President, Interfaith Dialogue Assoc. and Host of Common Threads: An Interfaith Dialogue, heard weekly on WGVU Radio, Grand Rapids, Michigan.

ABOUT THE AUTHOR

Mary Ann Johnston, author of *Sustained by Faith, Messages from Jesus* and *That Heaven*, is also a spiritual-living advisor, healer, and retired occupational therapist.

In 1945, when she was five years old, Jesus appeared to her as a radiant, ethereal being. Ever since that encounter, he has been a companion to her, giving her comfort and guidance throughout her life.

At the age of fifty, Mary Ann earned a degree in occupational therapy from Western Michigan University and then, in 1992, discovered she had a gift for spiritual healing and began integrating it into her personal life and occupational therapy work. Later on, she studied many healing modalities, but she still relies on intuitive promptings from Spirit to guide her when working with clients.

In 1998 Mary Ann had a profound awakening, which increased her awareness of divine realities, preparing her for what was to come. For, in 2002, Jesus encouraged her to write about her spiritual experiences and visitations from great beings, recording their words for humanity at this pivotal time in earth's history.

In 2005, in a near-death experience during a heart attack, Mary Ann visited the heaven she speaks of in *That Heaven*.

By sharing what she has experienced and received through the blessings of God, Mary Ann feels that she is helping others draw closer to God, increase the light in their soul, and realize their highest good—divine love and joy.

She teaches workshops and has been a guest speaker at churches in Michigan and the Southwest, speaking about spiritual living, healing, and her experiences with God and Jesus. She co-leads silent retreats at Song of the Morning Retreat, in Michigan, where she resides with her husband, George.

To find out more about Mary Ann Johnston and read a free chapter from *Sustained by Faith* or *Messages from Jesus*, go to: http://www.maryann-george.com.

www.ingramcontent.com/pod-product-compliance
Lightning Source LLC
Chambersburg PA
CBHW032059080426
42733CB00006B/335